The
Tucson Murders

The
Tucson Murders

◆

By John Gilmore

The Dial Press ✥ New York 1970

Library of Congress Catalog Card Number: 71-76970

Printed in the United States of America

First Printing, 1970

Designed by Terry Reid

For My Wife, Cecilia

Author's Note: THE TRIPLE

murder charges brought against twenty-three-year-old Charles Schmid, Jr., on November 10, 1965, resulted in one of the Southwest's most sensational murder cases. Its notoriety reached around the world. The desert community of Tucson was flooded with reporters, some from as far away as Paris and Tokyo. The pretrial publicity played so heavily on "the gruesome and sordid" aspects of the crimes that several of the reporters claimed it would be impossible to find an impartial jury in Arizona, or perhaps anywhere in the Southwest.

In early February, shortly before Schmid's first murder trial, I became involved in the case as a freelance journalist. The proceedings against Schmid were at once vague and complex. One reporter said, "The sensationalism has over-shadowed something important: Many facts of the case fit together like the pieces of a well-made jigsaw puzzle, while others seem to have come from a different box."

It was upon that concept that I felt a thorough presentation of the case would become necessary. But contradictions more inherent in psychology than in judicial matters focused my attention on the individuals accused and those who had been involved in the history of the murders. I believed that only through them could I perhaps *understand* enough to attempt to relate the events to a reader.

I became acquainted with Charles Schmid, Jr., on the third day of his first trial, and remained the only writer involved with him during that period of his life and the year to follow. All quotations attributed to him are taken from his diaries, letters, and memoranda transferred to me, and from our conversations over several months at Pima County Jail in Tucson, and on Death Row at the Arizona State Penitentiary in Florence.

I have attempted to follow the threads as a single story and present the picture as completely as possible. This book, then, is a reconstruction of that time in Tucson, and all material not derived from official sources, court proceedings, and actual occurrences is the result of extensive interviews and close contact with principals whose names appear throughout the text.

The names of a few individuals who played but a minor role in the cases have been changed. And to those other persons who have chosen to remain anonymous I wish to extend my appreciation for cooperation in the development of this book.

To two persons I am especially indebted, for without their confidence and generous assistance, this work could not have been undertaken. My most grateful acknowledgements go to Major Lois E. Hudson and Mr. Gary Greenberg, of Tucson, Arizona.

Tombstone, 1969   JOHN GILMORE

The
Tucson Murders

Part 1

ON THE MORNING OF November 10, 1965, a police car carrying five officers and detectives and a ninteen-year-old-boy drove along River Road, bordering the city of Tucson, Arizona, turned off on a narrow road called Pontatoc, and headed north into the desert. In the early light the land stretched out in sand-gray slopes, rocky, desolate, thick with catclaw and saguaro cactus. Where the asphalt ended pebbles rattled up in the fenders of the car. Trails rutted by countless car and motorcycle wheels branched away from the road like dried tributaries to disappear in the hills.

The boy said, "There's the radio towers."

Leaving the car parked on a trail, the policemen followed the boy past the radio towers through an area littered with empty beer cans, known to local teenagers as the Drinking Spot. Brush and old newspapers, caught by the wind, rolled against the men's legs as they hiked a short distance north. The area was strewn with cans, car parts, seats with jutting springs, punctured tires, junk, and strands of hair. The further they walked, the more hair they found; long reddish-blond hair, clinging to rocks and cactus. Skirting the junk piles, the boy finally stood on open ground atop a small hill; at his feet were disjointed bones and the upper half of a skull. The odor was heavy. A large black stain had spread over the ground in a rectangular shape and seeped into the sand like oil.

"That's Gretchen," the boy said, and as the policemen spread out he walked away, still staring at the ground.

A detective knelt and examined the skull. "This looks to me like it would be more like Wendy, don't you think?" he said, glancing up. The boy came back and looked down at the bones. He stooped, shrugged, stood up and again walked away. Further west he pointed out other bones, and the jawbone of the skull. Similar stains spotted the area and there were signs of digging, as though someone had attempted to shovel a grave in the hard-packed earth. It seemed apparent to the detective that the ground had proved too hard for digging, and that the corpse had been dumped there like the tin cans and car seats. And then the sun, the elements, and the animals had worked over the remains for months.

"Over here," the boy called. Down in a sandy wash

a second skeleton was lying under a mesquite tree, half-clothed in remnants of a jersey blouse, the knees raised and slightly apart. A pair of pin-striped capri pants were wrapped around one leg.

Richie Bruns, the boy leading the police, told them that the two skeletons were the remains of seventeen-year-old Gretchen Fritz and her thirteen-year-old sister, Wendy. He said that they had been killed by his closest friend, Charles Schmid.

◆

In 1942 a pregnant girl came to the Hillcrest Nursing Home in Tucson. She told the proprietors, Mr. and Mrs. Charles Schmid, Sr., that she was going to bear a child out of wedlock and did not want to divulge the name of the father. Arrangements were made for the Schmids to adopt the infant.

At eleven o'clock on the night of July 8, 1942, Charles Schmid, Jr., was born. The records of the birth, detailing the mother's identity, were sealed within an envelope and held in a Tucson bank, to be given to the child when he reached the age of twenty-one.

The nursing home around which Charles Schmid spent his childhood had been founded in 1921 by Charles Schmid, Sr.'s, mother. Schmid, Sr., was a native of Tucson, had attended Tucson High, and graduated in 1924. When he went to work for the fire department there was only one firehouse in Tucson, with one "shiny new fire truck."

When he married Katharine, a registered nurse from New England who came to work in the nursing home, Charles Schmid, Sr.'s, mother "a stern old woman with a will like tempered steel," did not approve of the marriage, "and the way Katharine was, big, determined, sometimes cold as ice, the two didn't exactly hit it off."

A sign outside the nursing home, a long whitish one-story building, reads OVER 31 YEARS' EXPERIENCE IN TUCSON. Across the street is a neat stucco house with a steel fence surrounding the property, and here the Schmids live. Next to it stands a smaller one-bedroom house with weathered siding and a green tarpaper roof. It has been on the property for over sixty-six years, and it became the "personal house" of Charles Schmid, Jr.

As a child, Charles Schmid was a trickster. His vivid imagination often overshadowed his abilities. A grammar-school teacher recalled her impressions of Schmid in the second grade: "He was an overly curious boy. He was brighter than most but seemed to be interested only in what he wanted to be interested in. The rest—like when you draw down a window shade."

Another teacher remembered that during his fifth year in grammar school she had been "at a loss to understand him *well*. His behavior was more than proper and he was one of the most courteous boys, he never caused any actual trouble . . . yet he was unreachable in a way." She said that often he would give "a below-average account of himself, not because he wasn't able to make more of what he was doing, but as though he just didn't care about it."

Schmid has few recollections of his early childhood. He has told friends that his foster father used to whip him at times, "apparently for no reason. . . . I hate him and he hates me. We can't even sit in the same room and talk about the weather without getting into an argument."

To one friend he confided that Katharine Schmid had told him that she had been in love "with a man that owned 200 suits." Schmid claimed that Katharine often spoke about the "wonderful man with 200 suits, how much she was in love with him," and he told the friend, "When the guy dies, I'll inherit the 200 suits."

"All I really remember about elementary school," he says, "was that I liked the people, but instead of the challenge of learning something new I'd race through assignments to be the first one done, it didn't matter whether I was right or wrong since I seemed to know the answers anyway. The feeling of this knowledge lying dormant gave me the weirdest sense of hallucinations. I'd shut my eyes and the logical solution would appear. . . ."

Schmid recalls that he "loved to run and run and everytime I ran I didn't feel frightened. I was very *very* frightened of being left alone and never went home from school on time because my parents were working and being so alone was dreadfully frightening.

"It seemed I always ran across busy roads, over walls

and into dangerous places where I was liable to be hurt. I didn't know whether this stemmed from a secret desire to hurt myself for attention, or simply because I just wanted to. When I received a bicycle I ran it off hills and down flights of stairs until we finally made a race track."

Paul Graff was Schmid's closet friend in elementary school. Paul's mother found young Schmid's behavior ". . . incredible. He would tell the tallest tales with such a clear-headed attitude that it made one sit in a trance. Then he would laugh and joke about it."

Schmid spent one summer riding bicycles with Paul Graff. "I won most all of those races because something inside me made me win. The times I'd lose was due to my recklessness."

Schmid enjoyed getting into mischief with Paul. "Paul was different and it fascinated me to be with him, but at times he frightened me at some of the things he'd want to do."

Paul and a friend named Roger once had an adventure that ended with their being sentenced to Fort Grant Industrial School for killing a man. It started with the boys running away from home with a .22 rifle. After buying some beans at El Rancho shopping center, they rode their bikes out of town and camped under a bridge the first night. The next day they hiked, shooting rabbits, and finally ate the last of the beans. They decided to try a holdup. "There just wasn't anything else to do," Paul recalls.

Roger lay in the road, pretending to be hurt, while

Paul flagged down a car. Finally an Air Force captain stopped to help them, and Paul thrust the rifle toward his face. "It had a hair trigger," Paul says. "I tried to lower it but I couldn't and it went off and hit him in the cheekbone."

"The guy started to spurt blood," Roger recalls. They dragged the body behind some bushes and hiked out to hide in the desert. By nightfall the sheriff's deputies found them. On the trip back to Tucson in the patrol car, Paul said, "Boy, this is going to be a big story. The biggest one this year. Wait'll you-know-who hears about this. He'll have to shoot two people to catch up with me."

◆

A San Francisco journalist traveling through Tucson in the late 1880s reported it as "a city of mudboxes, dingy and dilapidated, caked and baked into a composite of dust and filth." Some of those adobe hovels remain but the town has changed. From a population of 7,500 in 1900 (Tucson High's graduating class in 1910 consisted of nine seniors), Tucson today has over 309,000 inhabitants. The population more than doubled during World War II. In 1960 it was estimated that the population had grown at a rate of 368.4% over the previous ten years and since then it has quadrupled with subdivision after subdivision rolling out beyond the old city limits into Pima County, taking with it clusters of supermarkets and shopping centers.

Despite its high rate of growth, a bumper sticker stating: TUCSON WANTS INDUSTRY is a frequent sight. There are jobs in copper mining, agriculture, and a complex of air and missile facilities, but these are not enough to meet the demand for work. Many young people are unemployed and the prevailing wage scale is low.

Tucson's schools have failed to accommodate the city's large teenage population—a few of the high schools have devised a system of split sessions. One shift attends classes from 6:00 A.M. to noon, and another from noon until 6:00 P.M. Especially for those students with scholastic ambition, the broken routine presents problems. Many of the families have not lived in Tucson long enough to be considered residents and many leave within a year. There are large numbers of transients and drifters, families as ever-shifting as the desert surrounding Tucson. Their children have little ambition and show a high dropout rate.

A Southern Pacific folder in the 1890s announced that "Tucson receives the sick and sends them away every whit whole." The city has always been a refuge for the infirm, the sick, the disabled, and the retired. Hospitals, nursing homes, and rest centers form an essential part of Tucson's economy. The asthmatic and arthritic are attracted by the perennial sun and consistently dry air, for Tucson is a city surrounded by desert, an island of some eighteen by twenty miles with an elevation of 2,400 feet, situated in a broad valley bordered by mountains that rise from five to nine thousand feet.

Frequently people go out into the desert to commit suicide, and murderers to dispose of their victims. It is said that a corpse decomposes so swiftly in the desert that after six weeks it is hard to tell how long the body has been there. Old people in rest homes have wandered off, as though summoned from their beds, to be absorbed by the elements. One elderly man parked his car, placed his shoes and folded his jacket by the roadside, and walked into the desert. When found days later his body was already partially decomposed.

"Tucson is dead," the kids complain. For most of them—uninterested in school, unemployable—the desert takes nothing and offers nothing, but remains an encompassing burden. Life is a drag. "There's nothing to do." Every year over 600 teenagers disappear from Tucson, the majority of them girls.

"Downtown?" says a police sergeant, "hell, after dark you can roll a bowling ball straight through it and not hit a thing. Speedway's where the action is. That's where they go."

East Speedway: a long broad unzoned road reaching from downtown Tucson east across the city, fading into the foothills and cactus, crowded with drive-ins, hamburger havens, service stations, used-car lots, laundromats, and rock 'n' roll clubs. Female minors are admitted to places serving liquor, and boys can obtain false ID cards for around ten dollars.

"You got to have a hot-engine, bitchin' wheels," one boy says. "You cruise Johnnie's Drive-in, go around and come out, in the driveway then down Speedway and back again. Cruise Johnnie's some more or drive out to the desert. If there's no beer parties in the desert, there's always parties at someone's house."

♦

In high school, Charles Schmid was known as a gymnast. He was an indifferent student; most of his grades were D's. A home-room teacher says, "I did think he had exceptional intelligence but did not know what to do with it; there was no *guiding* line."

In 1960 Schmid led the school to the State Gymnastics Championship, winning the flying rings and still rings, placing in the long horse, and taking fifth on the horizontal bar.

According to Schmid, "I tried as hard as I could and made the tryouts for freshman football, but I couldn't express myself as an individual in football, so I quit. I wanted something that depended on my actions *solely*, and nobody else was needed to depend on. I decided on gymnastics. The weird and marvelous exhibitions fascinated me, so head over heels I plunged. I read books, studied techniques of famous gymnasts and then worked to build my body to suit the application. In one year the weird and mystic dream descended and made everything believable to me. I could do it, there was no doubt about it."

Repeatedly in Schmid's life, and as far back as he can recall, he has been aware of "seeing events" in his mind before they actually occurred.

He says, "I soon felt engulfed by the strange hallucination of knowing that I could do it, seeing myself doing it before it happened. The things that other gymnasts struggled months to achieve I accomplished in a matter of days.

"The first year I barely made the team, the second, third, and fourth I became city and then state champion. It is difficult for me to explain how I was champion for three years straight with only one semester of practice. All I can say is that whatever trick or event seemed impossible to others, I'd shut my eyes and everything would seem logical, so I'd do it. I wish I could honestly say I worked harder than others, but as I progressed everything seemed easier."

Schmid's foster parents had given up the operation of Hillcrest and opened Katharine's Craycroft Center, a luxurious, red-brick, multibuilding nursing home at a leased location on Craycroft. The old Hillcrest was in use as a boardinghouse for elderly people. Schmid had his own quarters in a sand-toned territorial house on the same property as the new nursing home, and since his sixteenth birthday he had been receiving an allowance of $300 a month. He had a new car and a motorcycle, and his foster parents were later to admit that they did not interfere in their son's life. Katharine felt that "Charlie had his own life to lead . . ."

As a fifth-year student, Schmid was no longer eligible

to compete in gymnastics. Just before graduation, he was caught taking some tools from welding class to work on a roadster he was building, and was temporarily suspended. He could have returned and graduated after a semester but he never asked to be readmitted. Schmid says: "I quit out of boredom." He started hanging around Speedway, drinking and picking up girls.

"Everyone knew who Smitty was," an ex-classmate recalls. "They all called him 'Smitty,' I really thought his name was Smith or something. He was a loner, he had a peculiar popularity, by that I mean the girls went for him, along with those that wanted to act like Smitty. He was strange and probably the most conceited person in Tucson, but he had a way of acting that excited people."

There were the rock clubs, the hangouts, the parties. The life along Speedway was important to Schmid and he once tried to describe what it meant to him. He wrote:

"A wild expressive mass jerks spasmodically to the liquid drums and pulsing sounds from the amplifiers. All the yes sirs and no sirs are absent, and an exchange of physical desire obscures the rancid reality around them. The hungry kisses accented by a pill or a few beers is a cheap and easy way to find security, and the quick, too-soon responses and climaxes insure protection from the outside world. The teenager is frightened beyond belief by the world he is being forced into. What sense is it to wait for sexual intercourse, he reasons, when it's available now? Why not take a pill, or get drunk, at least there is a happy void to fall into. All the doubts are still there but they're pleasantly obscured. All that matters is the good feeling you're getting from speed and intoxication. Granted, there are some kids who try to untangle the incredible mess, but how can they do it alone when the rest would rather sit in the corner smoking pot? . . . But why shouldn't they be disillusioned and find other worlds? All the pretty little tinsel and ribbons society wraps the box with to tantalize them in hopes they'll want it and try harder than ever, is just a fairy tale to conceal the dirty contents inside. The blind faith you try to project to seal the leaks is proving to be more and more fallible. It doesn't matter anymore if a button-happy idiot blows up the world."

◆

Richie Bruns, who was to become Charles Schmid's closest friend and most receptive ear for Smitty's philosophy, came to Tucson when he was in the fourth grade. His family made the trip from Columbus, Ohio, to the Southwest because both his father and older brother suffered from asthma. "My brother had it so bad he almost died when he was four," Richie says. He lived with his family in a modest house on Winsett, on the east side not far from the Schmids'. His father was an electronics technician and his mother was employed as a manicurist. Richie's brother, working for his master's degree at the university, had never been in trouble, but Richie was well known to the Tucson police by the time he was a freshman at Rincon High. It was around this time that he first saw Smitty. "He'd cruise down in his red convertible along the street between the main building and the cafeteria, and all the kids would come running out and gather around the car. He had his hair dyed black and he sometimes wore a sleeveless poncho or vest to show off his build, and wore engineer boots, the real tuff kind with buckles on the sides. Smitty was bitchin'."

Richie had been suspended or expelled from high schools four times before his eighteenth birthday. Then, during his second semester at Rincon, Richie quit school and began to spend most of his time around Speedway.

"I was hanging around the Coppa," Richie recalls. "They had these pinball machines there, and all you had to do to play was pick them up and drop them. It would rack up about ten games. I'd get there early in the morning and drop the machines and play them all day. Al Easton, who lived in back of the Coppa was going with Carol White. She'd hang around the Coppa and guys were on the make.

"Carol and Al broke up. I'd been spending days and nights at Al's house and I started to see Carol. I'd sleep with her and use Al's as an excuse, that I was staying over at his place. But I'd sneak out and go to Carol's. Al knew all about it and didn't care. He said fine. Carol had all kinds of brothers and sisters and no dad. The old lady was drunk and gone most of the time, whoring or getting on welfare, and Carol took care of the kids. She had to be mother at fourteen to all those brothers and sisters through the week with no money."

There was a motorcycle crowd around the Coppa; their bikes lined the front of the building. Richie would see Smitty around the Coppa. "He had a Harley CH," Richie says, "but he was not part of that crowd. Smitty played at being a bike guy, but the real bike guys didn't go for his games." Things were rough at that time, but Richie was "just a fifteen-year-old, one of those kids that hang around and look stupid. Even after they put up the NO LOITERING signs we'd just hang around."

Eventually, Richie began spending most of his time at Carol's. "Others would come by with booze and money for Carol, and she'd entertain and I would stay there all the time. It went on like that for about three months, the summer.

"At nights we'd lay out on the grass and look at the sky. I didn't care, it was like I didn't have parents. Nobody knew who you were, nobody came around or cared, and it was nice, laying out there and staring up at the sky. Sleep a little. It was paradise for a fifteen-year-old."

This came to an end. "One night I was staying with Carol," Richie says. "We were having sex on her front porch, it was a closed-in place, with the TV going. Carol had only her panties on, we were lying on the old couch out there and suddenly her old lady comes rushing up, shaking a .45 at my head. She'd been watching us through the screen. She was drunk and that .45 kept shaking in her hand, pointing right at my head.

"Later, Al, Carol, and I broke into a house and we got caught. Al's little sister saw us and told her old lady, who called the cops. I got put on probation then. They said I couldn't hang around Carol or Al ever again. I did anyway. After that they sort of cracked down on Carol and her family. Carol got sent to Good Shepherd up at Phoenix. After that I kept thinking about how I was going to see her, break into Good Shepherd and all that. I kept plotting and writing it all down, how I was going to do it. My old lady gave my writing to the probation officer and there was more trouble.

"I started working at the car wash and took off work one day and went to the Coppa. This faggot comes in and starts flashing this damned money and asks me if I want a beer. I said, 'Yeah, sure,' so I went out with him and he bought a six-pack. I really got wiped out of my mind. He drives out in the desert and starts proposing all this shit and I told him where to go.

"I'd told him I'd run away once and he told me how I could run away because he could pose as my old man. I said, 'Well, fine, let's go.' That was the last thing I remember until I woke up and was looking at some scummy side of town and I said, 'Hey, where the hell are we?' 'We're in Phoenix,' he said. 'Let's turn around and go back,' I told him. On the way back I start driving and the center line starts weaving and then we're in the ditch. He pulls me out and says, 'Cops saw that, cops coming.'"

When the police picked up Richie, he said "the queer showed me a gun," and the police let him go. But the incident wasn't over. "Next day the cops came and tell me a guy like the queer was found in a ditch on the scummy side of Phoenix, shot. They'd found him dead. They take me down to Mother Higgens [Juvenile Detention], apparently on suspicion of murder. Then I think they found the guy who killed the queer, but I got sent up to Fort Grant for breaking probation."

At Fort Grant, Richie remembers, "Eight people sit at a table, three bowls with main foods. The object is to grab a bowl and hold it up in the air when you are done. Some kitchen help comes around and picks up the bowls. There are so many bowls in the air, chances are you won't get to eat unless you grab fast as soon as grace is said. They can't wait, and just grab as soon as it's said and 'chop down.'"

◆

Schmid's school friend, Paul Graff, had just returned from Fort Grant. Schmid recalls, "Something in my mind clicked when Paul was released. . . . As his best friend, he came to me for help and nothing else seemed to matter." Schmid had broken off with one girl friend and had been invited to another girl's house for dinner.

He asked if he could bring his good friend along. The girl was reluctant, then said, "You better not tell them who he is or anything."

Usually adults were impressed by Schmid. He was courteous, attentive, especially to mothers, "full of life and energy," as one parent recalls. "There was something odd about him, the makeup, his hair dyed, but he'd explain that he was performing with a group, playing guitar, and he was every bit a gentleman."

The dinner was not a success. Conditioned by Fort Grant meals, Paul began grabbing and wolfing, as though his life depended on how much he could get into his mouth at once. Schmid says, "Paul was the most sarcastic person I had ever seen. It seemed impossible that Fort Grant had changed him so completely. His manners ruined the dinner and he was so rude to her parents we were asked to leave. That ended my visits to the girl's house."

On the street, Paul said he had nowhere to go. "He was just standing there," Schmid says, "the food still on his mouth, staring at the ground. I asked my parents if he could stay at our house, they said yes, so he moved in. During this time I was involved with several girls, and with cars (the roadster I put together turned 135 inside of three blocks), and with practicing the guitar and taking singing lessons from a woman coach in Tucson. I just really wasn't attracted to the kind of life Paul had been used to. He was just burning with a hate for everything and he was doing some extremely heavy drinking."

They drove down to Nogales. Smitty wanted to order custom-made shoes and also look at some jewelry. "I told him not to buy any booze because we'd get caught smuggling it across the line. But when I'd gone to the bathroom Paul bought three big bottles of tequila, hid one of them in the glove compartment and the others in the rear trunk. When we were questioned at the border, I said we didn't have any liquor. He didn't believe us and made me open the trunk and then another one looked in the glove compartment.

"My car was impounded and it was to cost me $20 to get it out. Paul had $35 but he wouldn't loan me the twenty. I had loaned Paul a hundred dollars while he was with me, given him a roof and free food and even got him some work at the hospital. We hitchhiked back to Tucson, and as soon as we arrived Paul packed his things and left.

"I was so disappointed I took a quart of Falstaff and drank it. Intoxication accented my feelings." But a week later Paul returned, offering apologies which were accepted lightly. There were other things on Smitty's mind. He was seeing a girl named Sandy. She was married. He'd also been designing some automotive parts and had progressed to the point where a business venture seemed possible. He decided to go to California to purchase a furnace for an aluminum factory, so, with over $2,000 stuffed into the top of his boot, he went on his "business trip," thereby avoiding a confrontation with Sandy's husband.

He was detained by the Beverly Hills police on

suspicion of robbery, but was released when the $2,000 in question was accounted for. For several days he stayed in Los Angeles, and was later to say that he'd spent the time with an "L.A. whore who taught me some tricks." He returned to Tucson, and the business venture, like other enterprising schemes Smitty would hit upon from time to time, failed to materialize.

◆

After six months at Fort Grant, Richie Bruns was released. "The first thing I did was go back to the bowling alley. The first hour back I was with Rus and the other guys." At the Coppa or Rollerama he'd see Paul, "a wino, who had to have a drinking companion like every other wino, and I'd drink with him." Through Paul he got to know Smitty, and they started going out every Saturday night. "We'd hang around the Coppa, then split with a case of beer in the trunk, and go out to the desert, park, shit around. If Smitty wanted to stay in the Rollerama, it was me and Paul, Paul drunk on wine. We'd drive Smitty's car and I'd bum chugalugs with him."

Other nights, Richie would take a motor scooter he had "acquired" at the time, drive to the Coppa and drink with whoever was there, and then go to Rollerama, "strictly Smitty's crowd," where he'd circulate among the drinking groups or "just hang around." Most of the time he didn't have enough money to go inside so he and Paul would stay outside with the drinking groups. Richie recalls: "They'd have Chuck Berry, Fats Domino, Bill Black combo, and draw quite a crowd. But all the juvenile delinquents would be hanging around in the parking lots and I was one of them." There were frequently fights with cops, deputies arresting kids, and, "Every week the Liquor Control would crack down."

Schmid often went into Rollerama to get a girl. "He'd take her out to the desert by the Apache Drive-in," says Richie. "Paul and I would wait. Many nights I waited while Smitty was with some girl in her bedroom." There was a girl named Sue Nemer for a while and, according to Richie, "Her old man never liked Smitty, it was something right off from the beginning. When Smitty broke up with her, Paul started making it with her and Smitty didn't like it. He couldn't go in the pad and found himself in the position of waiting on Paul (instead of Paul and I always waiting on him—many times we'd been there waiting when Smitty'd come running out, 'Get the hell out,' with his clothes in his hand, charging out through some chick's bedroom-window screen). He didn't like being in that position, of waiting for Paul, so one night when Paul was in there with Sue, Smitty went to Mr. Nemer's car and disassembled the engine on the car port, laid it out in parts. Paul got blamed and Mr. Nemer threatened to shoot Paul if he ever came near the house."

One particular night Smitty seemed "really quiet." He

was walking with Richie along Craycroft to Johnnie's on Speedway. Richie was quiet too, he was thinking of running away, of heading north. Maybe west.

They sat for a while on the brick wall by the driveway at Johnnie's. Richie told Smitty that he wanted to get on the move again.

"Smitty didn't say anything right away," Richie recalls, "Then he told me about his *real* old lady."

According to Richie, Smitty told him the following:

During a family upset at the Schmids', the grandmother revealed to Smitty that he was an adopted child. He refused to believe her and went immediately to Katharine. "Yes, that's true," his foster mother said. She took him to the bank and asked for the sealed envelope. She handed it to Smitty and said "you're old enough now to know, I suppose."

Then Smitty made a trip to Phoenix, and later told Richie that he had confronted the woman named in the envelope as being his real mother. Smitty said the woman told him "I didn't want you when you were born, or even before you were born, and I don't want you now. Get out." Smitty said she slammed the door in his face.

Art Meyers, a mutual acquaintance of Schmid and Bruns, remembers Richie as "kind of weird. The kids in school didn't think much of him, and they thought Smitty was a fruit, a creep. You see, Rincon is a twink school. It's pansy-like, all the guys wearing them wingtip shoes, saddle shoes, big ugly fat loafers, sandals, surfer hair style, I mean stuff like that. Forget it! I wouldn't go for that and we just dressed the way we liked to dress. Smitty and Richie, we all dressed alike, ascots and stuff like that, just trying to be different.

"A lot of kids, they didn't see you going along with the crowd, so they thought something different of you. But if they didn't like it—too damn bad! They can go to hell. We'd put on our go-to-hell ascots and go-to-hell shoes, and if they didn't like it, too damn bad. Richie wore suits and ties and even a topcoat in summer, and always wore shades.

"When Richie was in school, he even wore suspenders. Richie's not dumb at all. His older brother's a real clean-cut guy, goes to the university to be a teacher and Bruns has a complex. He has a pretty good home in a pretty good part of town, his old man was OK, his mom was OK, but Richie's juvenile trouble resulted from a complex. His folks gave his brother all the attention, everything went to his brother. And Richie, he had to do something. . . ."

In January of 1963, Richie was returned to Fort Grant, convicted on two counts of burglary.

While Richie was in Fort Grant—"The first time there I was scared, but the second time you know what the stakes are, when you'll get out, and that's it"—Smitty rented a house near 28th and Woodland with Paul and two other boys, Kenny and David.

There were other friends: Art Meyers, who played drums for a rock group Smitty fronted, and John Saunders. "Saunders started coming around to the house," Smitty says. "He seemed to like my music, and later

I got him a job at our hospital, gave him some clothes and a lot of my records. I tried to get girls for him. He dated but they didn't like him. I couldn't understand that because I always thought John was quite good-looking."

Slim, with a sensitive face, John Saunders was a poor student, constantly beaten, bullied, or teased by his classmates. An only child, he'd been afflicted as an infant with allergies producing scabs which encrusted his entire body. To keep him from scratching, his parents used to tie his hands and feet to the sides of his crib at night. Eventually he was cured of the allergy and the scars, but he had become so conditioned by the ropes that he couldn't sleep without being bound hand and foot. He developed asthma.

"Once when he was at the house," Smitty recalls, "something happened and John got into a fight with Paul, who hit him so hard he knocked him out. John didn't regain consciousness and Paul panicked. Finally he did become conscious but went into a catatonic stupor. We quickly invented a story that John fell off the roof. This was to keep Paul out of trouble as John was only seventeen and Paul was twenty-one.

"He (John) stayed at the hospital for a week recuperating. His parents knew he was there but they did not come to see him or offer to pay the medication bill."

One of the girls Smitty frequently went around with was Mary Rae French, sixteen. Mary had been living in Tucson only six months when she met Smitty. Her family came from Texas and occupied a modern beige house in the southeast section of Tucson. One of her teachers at Palo Verde High, where John Saunders was also enrolled, considered Mary, "a slow girl, given to lapses of daydreaming or simply staring into space. She couldn't keep herself down on any subject long enough for it to sink in. And before she dropped out of school, she had quite frankly developed a bad reputation for herself."

Schmid met Mary at a desert beer party. "Mary was so wiped out she didn't even know her name," Schmid recalls, "Later she was appealing to me because of the things she'd been through and I sort of understood. She had a terrible problem about speaking to people and a hypernervousness that made her stutter sometimes. On the first real date she got completely drunk and weeped out the history of her terrible family life.

"But she'd been hurt by so many things I think she hated the world. She had so many problems I don't believe she really knew what was going on around her. If she did she never showed it. Whenever I had friends over or fooled around and played my guitar, she was hostile and silent. I'd try to get her to socialize but her constant fear of people doing her wrong would end it. Yet, except for my never being true to her, we seemed to get along."

Schmid was having relations with a number of girls at the time. "Even though I was 'madly in love' with some particular girl at some particular time, as soon as I'd leave her I'd find another girl. I couldn't stand

being without a girl for even a moment, and as hard
as I'd try I couldn't be true. Each girl was something
new and different. I liked them all."

Smitty would propose marriage to several girls simul-
taneously, and at one period he took small amounts of
money from some of them. Under the impression that
he was going to marry her, Mary French accepted a
job Smitty had arranged at the hospital, and placed
her earnings in an account with him.

"I enjoyed being a gigolo," Schmid says. "Since I
thought I'd never fall in love anyway, going with those
girls and getting paid for it was my idea of fun. I had
sex, . . . money, and all I had to do was laugh or tell
a few jokes, which came naturally anyway. I also enjoyed taking girls from my buddies. Actually girls were
just a plaything at that time. I couldn't believe anyone
could take them as seriously as some others did. Life
was a funny joke full of phony people and if I couldn't
fight them I was damn sure going to join them and be
A-Number One phoniest.

"When I made a girl cry by going out with another
girl after I'd promised not to, I rationalized it by saying,
'Cry tonight and I'll make you laugh tomorrow.' It
sounded crazy but it worked. All the incredible lies
I told them. The wilder and more ridiculous the stories
the more they believed it as gospel. To avoid marriage
I told one girl I was part Negro and if we had a baby
it would be polka-dotted. I did it to get rid of the girl
but she really got determined to get married after
that.

"The story about my leukemia originated with some girl I was going with when I was seventeen. The purpose was to give her the impression I had a short time to live and would she be so kind as to make me happy by having sex with me. It worked so well eventually everyone believed I had leukemia. I was surprised at the speed the rumors spread. Only a few words assured me of success with sex.

"Other stories ranged from cancer of the heart to ten or twelve foster parents who had disowned me. Some had tried to sell me across the border for white slavery.

"I said that as a child my legs were all twisted and crippled and that was the reason I was so short, not to mention the operations performed on my pitiful limbs, or the elaborate stretching machine that had drained my family into poverty. Then there were sick brothers and sisters demanding money for emergency operations or burying stillborn children.

"One brother was insane and kept locked in a small room somewhere and I was his sole support. Some of the stories were of a more fantastic nature—that I'd flown jet planes during the war, and that I was the chairman of a secret organization that met at midnight for perverted sexual pleasures. Later on I was to tell a tale that I'd committed murder, shot a boy and buried him in the desert. I said the boy had been responsible for the death of a girl I loved, an automobile accident. . . . I said I cut off his hands before I buried him. So the extent I'd go for my girls was frankly unlimited.

To me, the fact that I'd actually be believed was the most incredible part of all. . . . I lived in a swirl of confusion but I didn't drown. Instead, the constant confusion gave me fire to want to live more."

It was Smitty's intention to get enough money together to cut a record. Art Meyers thought Schmid had talent. He recalls, "He was pretty good, pretty fair. We played at his house and over at my house a couple of times. He sings all right, he wanted to impersonate Mr. Elvis Presley. They do look alike, a little bit, the way Smitty combs his hair, his blue eyes, the sideburns. I told him once, 'You look like Elvis,' and he said, 'I can't stand the guy, I can't stand him.' The time we got together at his place, though, I went into his room and the walls were plastered with pictures of Elvis, records, pictures, photos. . . ."

But to Richie, Smitty was more candid. "Some people think I try to be like Elvis Presley," Richie recalls Smitty saying. "But the fact is that Presley's a creep—I don't even *like* the guy. But he's setting the *pace* and in order to *make* it, I'll have to cut a record—and it'll be better than Presley, except that he's setting the pace, the way I want to go to make it good." And Smitty was studying Presley's songs, manners, singing along with Presley and taping the voice.

Smitty says, "I found I couldn't sing and play lead guitar both so I taped my guitar playing over and over until I had it perfect. Then I recorded about thirty songs on my tape recorder and concealed my recorder in my specially made amplifier. At parties I could sing

and play lead guitar the way I wanted it and still joke
and cut up, without having to worry about making a
mistake playing. I faked the playing perfectly. But one
party, I remember, the cord came out of my guitar and
to this day there is a girl wandering around out there
who can't figure out how my electric guitar played
without a cord. I told her some idiotic thing I dreamed
up.

"The bass, rhythm, and drums could never figure out
how I played so perfectly. It was a blast joking everybody. I'd sit around and crack up for hours over it.

"Occasionally for laughs I'd tape some extremely
difficult song, some guitar player (who'd played professionally for fifteen or twenty years) had done, and
I'd fake playing it at a party and sing also. People
couldn't believe it. I practiced for hours in front of a
mirror, it was a ticklish delight for me to pull it off so
beautifully. I'd never overdo it, so no one caught on.

"Later, after the trial runs, I put controls on the
guitar itself to control the starting and stopping of the
recorder, also the tone and volume. Was life ever one
big happy blast.

"My voice had always sounded all right, at least to
me, so I never really gave a damn whether anyone
liked it or not. I liked it; so far as anyone else goes, it
doesn't really matter."

Schmid's music and half-baked plans for fame revealed the same insincerity as did his romances. He
tried to arouse sympathy by his tales of ill luck or shortcomings, to convince others that he was a cripple, in-

curably sick, or morally debased. Although Schmid passed this off as a tactic which he repeated only because it was successful, he admittedly had little concern for the girls themselves. One of them says, "Some girls went out with him just to see what he was like, he'd win them over and then be on his way. And still they didn't know what he was like. . . ."

Mary French, who was so "out of it" that she hardly seemed to know what was happening, was merely an extreme example of Smitty's girls, all of whom tended to be "lost," a group apart, seeking in some way to be different, to challenge.

Smitty was different, they said. It didn't matter that he stuffed his boots with rags and pieces of folded cardboard to make himself appear taller. It didn't matter that he wore makeup, dyed his hair, and was "disliked by most kids." In fact it seemed to make him more important. And among those that sought his company he was a leader. "Everyone knew Smitty." He had money, wheels, a pad of his own, and most important "he did whatever he wanted to do."

◆

There was a band playing at a new shopping center, and Richie, released from Fort Grant, wandering around, saw Smitty "racing around with John Saunders," then saw him later at the bowling alley. Richie says, "The old Coppa group had completely split up. The real bad guys were either married or in prison."

The juvenile problem at Rollerama had resulted in
its being temporarly closed down.

One afternoon Richie was walking to the bowling
alley when Smitty drove by and stopped and picked
him up. Smitty had a new bronze Ford Falcon, but he
complained that Katharine had cut off his allowance
temporarily, due to financial troubles at Craycroft.
"Things were rough," Richie says. "He didn't have any
money and was restless as hell. We got to talking about
some of the people we knew—Paul was laying some
girl and thought she was pregnant, and we talked about
John Saunders. . . ."

In order to get money from his foster mother, Smitty
obtained enrollment papers from the university and
convinced her that he would be attending classes, "although he bought no books, no texts, nothing," according to Richie. Smitty would occasionally wake Richie
up at 6 A.M. "First thing in the morning I'd hear his
car outside and then his boots crunching the gravel,
then bang-bang-bang on my bedroom window. Sometimes the goddamn sun wasn't even shining yet."

They'd talk. Smitty kept a toothpick in his mouth
and would work it around casually as he spoke. At
times he sat with a clothespin fastened to his lower
lip. Both lips were often so heavily covered with Chap-
stick that they appeared whitish and wet. He began
wearing darker makeup on his face, or Man-Tan. A
slight mole on one cheek was accented with a black
pencil.

Richie says, "The makeup got progressively worse

as time went on. And the mole, it started out a little teeny thing, it kept getting bigger and bigger. I think eventually it would have covered the whole side of his head.

"He went out and got these boots he'd had made down in Nogales. These things were something else, black, laces all the way up the back, had a cowboy heel that comes way in and out, they looked just like the old shoes that you see these old women used to wear years and years ago with the lace coming up the back. And the pointed fronts, and then he'd put the rags in them and his feet were real wide, coming way out on the sides. Paul looked at them one day and said, 'What's happened to him? He looks like a clown.'

"I was embarrassed. He had laces up them and straps coming across the instep, square straps with lace, then laces all the way up the back, real long things with all kinds of knots, big knots tied all the way down. Big long cowboy heel that came in too much at an angle, and the things came out real boxy to points on the toes."

Smitty often stared at his transformation in the rearview mirror of his car. Richie says, "He was constantly admiring himself in the mirror, pursing his lips, checking his eyes, touching his face here and there like a girl. The rearview mirror was so twisted around in that position that it wouldn't work in any other position. It just kept falling down."

With nothing else to do, Richie spent most of his time with Smitty, once in a while with Art Meyers, who remembers, "We played pool a lot, we were pretty close. Not too many people got along with Richie, he's a little off his cord, I know that, but he's a real comical guy. And Smitty is like that too, a real comical guy. So their characters were sort of combined. That's why they got along so good, once upon a time."

Richie recalls, "Smitty never liked to go on a date alone. One thing about him, he hated to go on a date by himself. He always had to double with somebody. He had to make an affair out of everything. He just *couldn't* go out with a girl alone. That's why I doubted all his bullshit about who he'd fucked; with practically every girl's name mentioned, he'd say, 'Oh, I fucked her—I fucked her.

"He especially liked to double-date if he knew the other guy was with a girl he knew he had control over. If he had two girls along that dug him, he'd be the center of attention, plus he talked a lot, and made with all the jokes. He talks and talks and is the center, doesn't shut up for a moment from the minute he meets a girl's parents."

Except Mary French. Richie says, "She wasn't like all the other schoolgirls. Anytime he wanted to, Smitty could just go around to Mary's, knock on the window at three in the morning or so, and she'd let him in."

Although Richie would double-date with Smitty, he says, "Me, when I go out alone, I mean, I got along better by myself. I can't do anything in a crowd. As soon as I'm in a crowd I completely shut up. That's why I never got along in school. I become somebody in the corner. I can't go into a strange crowd and make friends, like Smitty does. He had the ability to go around strangers and start talking, joking, making friends. I never was that way."

In fact it was Smitty's easy manners that Richie felt so drawn toward. Plagued by tensions and constant dissatisfactions, ashamed of his thinness, Richie was in many ways Smitty's antithesis. "Nothing bugged Smitty," Richie would say with envy, his success with girls was nothing like Smitty's.

Schmid remembers: "Richie once asked me how I turned on a girl to interest her in having sexual relations. He was having such rotten luck.

"I told him my routine with this girl named Beverly, my getting her into the bedroom, telling her a few jokes, making her a vodka collins and getting her in a laughing mood. Then I laughed with her and started tickling her. We fell back on the bed and I kissed her hair, forehead, cheeks, lips, and nibbled her ear lobes. I frenched her ear and the roof of her mouth with my tongue. I kissed her feverishly and with heated passion. She started to come back with her tongue and that's when I went into Act Two.

"I got up very quickly and sat on the edge of the bed. She said, very excitedly, 'What's wrong?' I looked at her and pretended to be very sad and hurt. 'Are you sick?' she asked.

"I looked even more sad and hurt and turned my head from her. She was shocked out of her mind. While my head was turned I conveniently dabbed some salt in my eyes. I had some in my shirt pocket. This caused a release of water which simulated tears and then I looked at her. She was taken off balance when she thought I was crying, and asked why. It was then that I'd tenderly take her hand and rattle off some tender garbage that would always come to me at such times. It went something like this:

"She'd say, 'What's wrong? Why are you crying?'

"'Darling,' I'd say, 'the tears I cry aren't tears of pain, they're tears of happiness. Never, no, never, have I seen someone as beautiful as you are right now. How could I be so fortunate as to kiss you tonight?'

"Then I'd kiss her hand very softly and tenderly and say, 'As I kissed you this moment I must certainly have kissed an angel because never before have I felt so . . . so clean inside.'

"Then another kiss, further up the arm, more garbage, more kisses, more poetic crap, more kisses, finally a kiss on the lips and then I'd promise never to leave her and I'd fight dragons etcetera all for her. All this crap took about an hour. . . . Oh, the crap I'd go through to set this up was very precise. Proper music, gobs of flowers, a wine bottle.

"This wine bottle was a special item. I spent twenty-five dollars for a vintage 1900 wine bottle, empty of course, and then I'd fill it with anything available—cheap wine, champagne, even beer once—and then seal it with wax. Then when she arrived at my house for dinner I'd break open the bottle and she was very impressed at the expense to make her happy.

"Damn, were they gullible. My worst problem was to keep from laughing. When I'd get caught laughing I'd simply say I laughed because being with her made me so happy.

"From there I'd go to the bedroom, usually to dance. My stereo was in the bedroom and it was more convenient to dance in the bedroom so records could be changed. One thing would lead to another. . . .

"The dinner and dancing would often come after a wild, exhausting night of dancing or running through the rain (very romantic, that rain). This would make them tired and set the mood. After the poetic garbage, tears, and pledges of devotion, about an hour or two of preliminaries would occur until I was positive the height of passion had occurred. Then I'd very discreetly disrobe her.

"I learned a very good technique to undo buttons and brassiere straps from a whore in California. Very seldom would the girl know her blouse and brassiere were disconnected until soft kisses sent her the message. Then my mouth, tongue, and kisses would probe other areas. This combined with more intimate caresses would virtually assure the completion of sexual intercourse.

"Well, after Richie heard about this with Beverly he decided to give it a whirl. But he drank too much and the girl slapped him."

◆

After a night of drinking and driving around, Bruns

and Smitty would often park in the nursing-home driveway, and Smitty would talk. Richie remembers it as "talk about God and stuff like that. About society . . . about what goes on in a girl's head. What does a girl want? He kept telling me, 'What are you going to offer a girl—you going to say I offer you my love?' What is love? He'd say, 'Nobody loves anyone. They want security.'

"And he'd say, 'God must be up there enjoying Himself because this all has to be nothing but a game, and we have to be little puppets and I resent having to be a puppet. And I'm supposed to love Him more than I love anybody, more than anything else, and He hasn't got the guts to show me His face. If I loved somebody, I wouldn't send him to hell for all eternity, whereas God would, so God isn't a kind God, but a cruel God, and all the Christians are the ones that have the plague thrown down on them. You say you love God, so He throws a plague down to test your so-called love. It's just a big game to Him, look what He did to His own son. God must be a hypocrite, He's a jealous God, and jealousy is a fault. God made me, and if I'm imperfect it's because He made me imperfect, so therefore God can't blame me for anything I do wrong; it's His fault.' "

Smitty had an abiding interest in this pseudo-theologizing. He says, "I had an incredible urge to read everything I could about philosophies and religion. When I was younger my parents took me to church every Sunday, but everything the preacher said about God sounded so much like the Easter Bunny. I distinctly recall thinking to myself, what will happen when all the grown-ups find out the preacher is lying just like they lied to me about the Good Fairy and Santa Claus.

"After I'd read something and it would conflict with what I'd been taught, I began to have doubts about everything. The booze and the girls had a numbing effect on these doubts."

Schmid read Epicurus and also "the various agnostic doctrines, esthetes and hedonists. The ones that seemed to me the most logical were the agnostics, even though the hedonists made the most sense. The stoics suffered too much but I thought their concepts were good. I'd learned that most people would rather exist in a fairy tale—I thought I wanted truth, if not that, then at least I wanted happiness. If everything was based on a pleasure-pain cycle, then I chose to receive more pleasure than pain. I gave my mind to seeking answers on its own. Involvement with pleasure seemed far more sensible than fighting a losing battle with rules and regulations. All the people I knew just sat back and said, 'Wow, it's happening,' but I had to know how and why, and I read everything I could.

"But I knew I was cynical about it. It appeared to me that I was sometimes adrift on an ocean of uncertainties and my anchor permanently entangled in a seaweed of frustration. Then suddenly before the drowning waves of accusations destroyed me, a lifeboat of cynicism preserved in laughter would rescue me. Somewhere in the depths of me this bubble of mockery prevails under the most excruciating circumstances."

Smitty could not take things as seriously as Richie did. Smitty was searching for pleasure, and it was not that rules and regulations were in opposition to that search, more that they were at times an interference. The "rules and regulations" did not really exist for Smitty. His life was being lived one segment at a time, while Richie, worrying over Smitty's soliloquies, began to notice things:

"Smitty and I were on the outside looking in. We'd walk into a restaurant and everybody looks at us like we're something from Mars. But they're actually afraid of us because we represent a threat to them. Actually, they're nothing but puppets themselves, and they know it, and they haven't got any self-respect. It's an imitation world. Everybody's phony, full of phony ideas and phony attitudes, phony principles."

Smitty, determined to be different, to be *himself*, stood out from the crowd. "I wasn't made to go through life at twenty-five miles an hour. I've got an awful lot of living to do before I'm too old to run upstairs without getting winded. Something, man, something too powerful inside me drives me and makes me different. I have to wear different clothes, I have to wear different shoes that I've designed, I've got to make my car different and I have to be different and I want to be. . . .

"I can't be a puppet or do what everybody else does. . . . I don't have any cause or rebellion—most people want to be alike. I don't. I want to be an individualist.

I might be one of the last to do and express what I feel. I'm going to have doubts about life and the existence of God until someone proves different. I can't accept all the crap and hypocrisy I hear about Jesus and God. . . . My basic logic tears apart the contradictions of today's religions."

What seems to have been Schmid's alone, made Charles Schmid into Smitty, and what led him to do what he had to do, was his insecurity—which was vast. He felt that he would never shake it. Already an immense gulf separated him from his foster parents.

Although he spoke of "an incredible raw wildness that refuses to lie dormant . . ." as having broken his life into a series of free-wheeling moments designed "to receive more pleasure than pain," he knew that his style of life was derived from insecurity. And this was driving him toward destruction, the "duels with Death and his disciples," toward some final liberating act which he supposed would somehow end the chaos he could not understand.

He wrote later, "I tried to cram as much experience into my life as possible. The basic wild and uninhibited attitudes have always originated from a fear of insecurity. Long ago it became accepted to my reasoning that everything in the world exists on a temporary basis only. I resented it and it accounts for the constant frustrations I endure. . . . Without something to tax my brain of its currents of anxiety I was not happy. I hated ruts and the constant monotony of life. I grasped and challenged head-on. . . . Experience has complemented my originality and forced it to project itself in countless channels—the set patterns and formalities I violate in search of this originality, constantly I searched and devised original plans of action."

One of Schmid's earliest memories was of trying to gain attention by recklessness, something that would hurt him, that he would later link to preoccupation with God's punishing him. He preferred a God who punished to a God who wasn't there. The great fear was of being abandoned in a world that was indifferent to him. It was better to arouse hostility than indifference.

Schmid wrote of the feeling of being alone and the fright it awakened in him. "The uncertainties of tomorrow and the lost yesterdays add tangible fuel to my inner rebellion. I honestly feel I was cast into the wrong period of time by some quirk of fate. My deepest recollection is that of actual vagueness to time. . . . My earliest memory is of surging over a deep pool of water when I was five. The experience is strikingly clear, even today. That was the first taste of fright and it became thrilling and compelling. Perhaps this cast the mold for future events. . . .

"I honestly wish I could channel the furies of my mind and body into a constructive field, but boredom of everything I try causes loss of appeal. . . . On a motorcycle or in my roadster at 120 miles per hour the world seems so damn appealing—the ecstasy of wind, noise, and the possibility of some unknown element casting disaster in my path, to test my physical and mental dexterity and the speeding-up of events causes a tremendous release similar to sexual orgasm. With any reduction of speed life becomes a reality and catches me, to subdue me in its boredoms, frustrations, and other complexities. The extreme speed and dangers frighten me but paradoxically stimulate me as well.

"I truly wish I could be a great surgeon, or philosopher, or author, or anything constructive, but in all honesty I'd rather turn my amplifier full-blast and listen to the noise until I'm enveloped. . . . Lovemaking combined with animal passions and a hint of cruelty as I reach sexual fulfillment is far more basic and sensible than the involvement with some theoretical manifestation that later proves itself not so absolute after all."

Themes of self-destruction were repeated throughout Schmid's life. Of his gymnastic ability, he wrote, "The thing that kept me fascinated with gymnastics was that it frightened me. If I slipped or fell that could very well be the last time. Each trick I did became more and more daring and I was tempted to let go just to know if I really would let go.

"It was a paradox, all my life I'd hated and feared to be alone and what occurred to me was that in gymnastics I was tempting injury or death which was surely solitude. I think I wanted to find out if anyone really cared. If it really mattered one way or the other. I enjoyed gymnastics because I was afraid. But during my last year of high school I quit gymnastics completely. I knew if I continued my recklessness would hurt me.

"Once, at Sabino Canyon, I almost drowned. There

was a storm and the creekbed rose with the oncoming rush of water. For an unknown reason I accepted a dare to jump across the torrent." (Richie and some others were there at the time.) "I missed by at least ten feet, but instead of screaming for help this incredible laughter prevailed. I was swept downstream and this maniacal laughter continued. I found myself actually enjoying the predicament and the feeling that I was completely helpless, that my fate depended on nature, was extremely exciting. . . . Fast speed and music provide an excitement similar to that incident. Pleasure, laughter, and excitement emanated from most every situation I undertook. Then came skydiving and the motorcycle.

"Before my motorcycle accident, one summer I saw a hurricane that seemed to have great meaning. From the murky sky there came a flash of lightning, white with heat as it greedily devoured a whirlpool of liquid turbulence to combine in a cyclopean monster. Hungrily it ripped everything from the face of the earth.

"I stopped the engine in horrid fascination as I tried to overpower the temptation of joining in the raw power. Sometimes I get so close and I can grab the surprise package and rip the covering to view the contents, it goes a little higher or farther away and I'm lost again. But I go a little faster, just a little faster, and there it is again and I'm close, real close. So I edge over that point of no return and I can't come back again, so I make a last grab and life jumps back and away and laughs as I plunge into darkness. The skydiving frightened me to such an extent that I knew I had to try it."

North of Tucson, Smitty made the required five static jumps, but on the sixth one, a free fall, he recalls, "As I was waiting to jump the wind blasted by and soaked me in its freedom. The approach zone came nearer and I had the desire to shed my clothes completely and spring off the perch naked of any guilt or inhibition. It was tempting. I jumped prematurely from the plane's ladder and laughed as they screamed to wait.

"After I waited the allotted five seconds to pass, I no longer wanted the parachute to open. It was one of the strangest feelings of my life. I was enraptured and kept falling, wondering if they were screaming down there, or what. The air rushed by and filled my lungs with crystals of fright, yet the fright acted as an explosive fury to rack my body with a thousand sensations. Each heartbeat increased the sensation. I was attaining an incredible orgasm, almost totally sexual, falling helplessly. . . . All my mind could register was that no one could go faster and I was quickly leaving the whole God-damned phony, rotten insecurity behind me, the fairy-tale world of stupidity, and since they created it, I wasn't really part of it anyway, nor did I really want to be. . . .

"I imagined I heard the spectators' screams, pleading, and that made absolutely no sense. Why should they care, why did they want me in their world at that precise moment; I tried to accept and believe what they believed, it was just that this driving fury dominated me. . . .

"There was no sensible reasoning behind their motives. Was it the conscience inside straining too hard that merited their actions? Isn't conscience a learned reaction based on environment, man from his most primitive surroundings had to find something to worship. Is it because all the uncertainties horrify him to such an extent he's in constant fear of loneliness and despair? Something kept pounding inside me to wait, I was going faster than anyone could and the whole rot-the mixed-up world was left behind. I was gone, I was like drunk and could decide my own fate. I'd been tempted not to open the chute but I did. . . .

"Many, many nights after that I lay awake wondering if I jumped alone would I open the chute in time, if I sensed no begging, pleading eyes around to penetrate my mind and cause me to rescue their consciences. And I knew I couldn't go back, that the temptation not to pull the parachute open would eventually win."

In this parachuting incident, Schmid ran through all the themes relating to his "duels with Death and his disciples." Again tempting somebody or something—other people, nature, perhaps God—to see if they cared enough to stop him from killing himself. Schmid was convinced that ordinarily they didn't. Reality, day-to-day living, is that "God-damned phony, rotten insecurity," the world they—other people or God—created that "I wasn't really a part of. . . ." And again, the danger drew attention to Smitty; there was constant exhibitionism in all of Smitty's bizarre acts. In the free fall, since he was falling through the sky he had to imagine what other people were doing, but he was fairly certain they were pleading with him, screaming for him to pull the ripcord.

All the escapades were shadowed by death, the only real certainty to end the "constant fear of loneliness and despair." He sought to drive himself beyond the ordinary, to some final confrontation which would end his isolation.

He never quite reached the point of suicide. "From the chambers of complexities in my soul, I called upon a strength to omit the thought of suicide. But the emptiness within my heart was too resurgent . . . I meditated on the decision of my death when suddenly an icy blackness paralyzed my actions."

But if he was not finally ready to kill himself he found ways to make the world pay attention. If they wouldn't love him, they might hate him. If he couldn't kill himself, he might kill others.

In a tight corner, Smitty described how he felt. He wrote: "I feel so alone and abandoned as if I were cast somewhere in the midst of my childhood again. I feel as if I were a mountain among mountains, only my mountain stood alone and frightened, ever attacked by the wind and the elements. On one side there is a steep perpendicular wall of black wet rock, streaked by ice and snow. No neighboring peaks protect this wall which stands exposed, ever covered with snow, attacked by the wind, oppressed by the overbearing weight of blue ice and boulders made heavier by the glistening shells of white crust, attacked by the leverages and pressures greater than any mountain can resist forever.

"My mountain bore the oppressive weight and resisted the leverages of the normal rhythm and tension of earth, rock, snow, and ice, until in one second of one hour of some day there could be added the one snowflake, drop of water, or mote of dust, and because of this infinitesimal disturbance the precise measure of a balance and rhythm would be torn free, and an avalanche of snow, ice, boulders, and valley-rending sounds would be torn loose from the mountain wall and take with it, in its plunge toward destruction, the bowels torn from the body of the sheer wall, to make more dreadful the blind engulfment, destruction, and burial of the good and the bad, the evil and innocent, no matter who or what lay in the path of the avalanche."

There came a time in the spring when the avalanche at last began to move.

Part 2 ONE NIGHT IN MAY

1964 a young girl disappeared. Her name was Alleen Rowe, she was fifteen years old, a sophomore at Palo Verde. She lived on Calle Cuernavaca, four doors away from Mary French. She was friendly with Mary but they were different: Alleen was a sensitive, above-average student who spoke seriously of college, was fascinated with oceanography, reincarnation, Russian novels. She took long walks in the desert to gather unusual stones, and told a friend, "I love the desert, it makes me feel alive." Even when the rest of Tucson kept their windows up to escape the heat, Alleen liked to feel the sun and know that she was part of the desert. "Everything becomes alive," she said. Yet at other times, infected with an adolescent melancholy, she'd dwell on thoughts of death, often discussing mortality with her mother, a registered nurse on night shift at the Tucson Medical Center.

Mrs. Norma Rowe had brought her two sons, Alleen, and a small brown dog to Tucson less than a year before. Although her house was somewhat older and not as large as the project houses on Calle Cuernavaca, Norma thought it had more personality. There was cactus and small cuttings arranged in flowerpots along the east wall. The sea shells, some spindly shrubs, and odd-shaped stones distinguished it from the project houses.

As a divorcee, Norma Rowe faced a number of difficulties and life was "not an easy chore." She had few friends in Tucson, but was close to her daughter Alleen, and mother and daughter considered themselves "friends." Norma didn't want any walls between them, but recently a certain distance had developed. Alleen had been seeing a boy from the university and he had given her his ring. Norma approved of the student, but was less sure about some of the others Alleen knew, like Mary French. . . .

At fifteen, Alleen had soft blond hair, made more yellow by the sun, framing the pleasant oval of her face. Her sea-blue eyes were bright and alert. Notwithstanding her age, she was more a woman than a child, and she told her mother all about her conversations with Mary, talks that dwelt heavily on sex. Mrs. Rowe didn't approve but Alleen defended Mary. "Alleen used to come giggling to me about all the things Mary

French had told her that day. 'You should hear her talk,' she used to say. And when I asked her why she listened, Alleen said she thought Mary was a nice girl. Alleen was so full of mercy that it never occurred to her that anyone would harm her."

The temperature on Sunday, May 31, 1964, stayed near ninety throughout the day. After dinner, wearing a black bathing suit and rubber sandals, Alleen watched the Beatles on television. It was still too warm in the house. She had planned to study for exams the following morning. She had to be at school by six A.M. But she grew sleepy as the balmy night closed in.

Shortly before nine o'clock, while Norma prepared to leave for work, Alleen took a bath, set her hair in curlers, then climbed into bed.

Norma announced she was leaving for work and entered Alleen's room. Her school books were laid out on the table by the bed, along with her purse. Alleen was lying on her left side the way she usually slept, her left arm partially over her right shoulder. In the dim light, Norma saw the metal curlers in her daughter's hair. She said good night and closed the door slightly. It was a few minutes after nine when Norma left for work.

Earlier that afternoon, Alleen had been talking to Mary in front of the French house. Both girls were standing near the curb when a bronze Ford Falcon approached on Calle Cuernavaca. Smitty brought the car to a stop at the curb. John Saunders was with him and there was another boy in the rear seat.

When Mary came to the car, Smitty said, "Get Alleen to go out with John tonight." While Smitty waited, Mary talked to Alleen. After a few minutes, Mary returned to the car and told Smitty Alleen couldn't go.

Alleen started home and Smitty drove off. Mary went inside. "Smitty called a little later," Mary recalls. "He told me to call Alleen and get her to go out with John. . . . He called four or five times more." Mary called Alleen three times, asking her to go out, that they'd double-date. But Alleen said she couldn't go.

Before dinner, Alleen was at a house nearby with a friend who was baby-sitting, and Mary went over and talked to her again about the plans for that night. Then Mary returned home. It was about eight o'clock when Smitty arrived with John Saunders.

Mary knew that Smitty had more on his mind than a double date. Some time before that night, Smitty had talked about "killing someone." He'd told Mary, "I want to kill someone. I want to kill a girl." He wanted to see what it would be like and if he "could get away with it." He had prepared a list of names, candidates for killing. One was Alleen Rowe.

It was almost eight o'clock. Smitty had John in the car when he came to Mary's house. Mary says that Smitty then told her that "He wanted to kill someone and that he wanted to do it tonight and asked me if I would try to talk Alleen into going out with John. He said that he would hit her with a rock and bury her in the desert." When Mary complained that she had tried repeatedly to get Alleen to go with John and failed, Smitty said, "If you can't get Alleen, get someone else."

Mary called a few other girls but none of them would go out with John. Smitty left and Mary returned to the house where Alleen's friend was baby-sitting, and she again spoke to Alleen about going out with John.

Finally, Mary says, "Alleen went home and she called me from her house and told me that she would go out with him . . . but she couldn't leave until her mother went to work."

Smitty returned to the French house, alone, and Mary told him Alleen would go with them. They'd have to wait until after her mother left. Then Mary accompanied Smitty to John's house.

"John and Smitty got a shovel," Mary says, "and put it in the trunk of the car. . . . I saw them take it out later." They drove around for a while and "drove by Alleen's house but her mother's car was still there. We just drove around . . . kept driving by until the car was gone." Then they parked by the alley at the Rowe house.

"I got out," Mary recalls, "walked up through the alley, and tapped on her bedroom window." A few moments later, "She came out the back door. She had on a bathing suit and shift. Her hair was in curlers."

Alleen was barefoot and carrying a pair of sneakers. Mary got into the front seat alongside Smitty. "John and Alleen were in the back seat." They drove east along 22nd Street and turned off at Harrison Road, at the edge of the desert, barren, bleak. Mary had visited that wedge of sand near Golf Links Road many times in the past with Smitty, when they "got drinking." She says, "The four of us got out of the car. We walked down into the wash."

After walking for a while they found a place where they could be comfortable and sat down. They started talking. Mary says, "Someone mentioned the radio and Smitty asked me if I would go up to the car and get one. It was pretty far away. He said he would go with me, and we went up to the car. We had just got to about the top of the wash when we heard Alleen scream. 'She needs help,' Smitty said. He told me to get in the car and stay there and he ran back down. I went and got into the car."

According to Saunders, when Smitty returned to the wash, Alleen was pulling away from John. Smitty said, "What's happening?" but before either could reply, Smitty grabbed Alleen. He told John, "Put your hand over her mouth."

John attempted to keep her quiet while Smitty bound her arms behind her back. John recalls that Smitty was using a guitar cord and that Alleen was asking, "Why are you doing this? What's wrong?"

"Mary wants us to do it," Smitty said, "She hates you, Alleen."

"Why . . . I don't believe you," Alleen said, then John reports that Smitty led her further down into the wash. They stopped. John says: "Smitty told me, 'Take her bathing suit off.' But I couldn't get it all the way down. 'Her hands are tied—here,' I said, 'I can't get it down.'" Smitty then untied her and removed her bathing suit. He spread her shift on the ground and told her to "lay down."

Alleen was lying naked and Smitty told John, "Go ahead." John knelt down and tried to kiss her but Alleen was crying, so he got back up and said, "It's no good, I can't, Smitty, not the way she's acting now." Then Smitty told John, "Go take a walk."

John remained standing for a moment and Smitty said, "What are you waiting for?"

Off by himself, John smoked a cigarette until he heard Smitty calling, "John—John."

When Saunders returned to the wash, Alleen had her bathing suit back on and was adjusting the straps. When she saw John, Alleen turned away and walked further down into the wash. Smitty indicated for them to follow her, and both walked a few feet behind her. "Smitty picked up a rock and handed it to me," John says, "meaning for me to hit her with it. 'I can't,' I said to him and handed the rock back to him. . . . Smitty said, 'Go tell Mary to come down here.'"

Mary had stayed in the car. She recalls: "About thirty or forty-five minutes passed, until John came back to the car and said that Smitty wanted me to come back down."

John remembers that, "Mary was crying. . . . I said, 'Smitty wants you to come back down there.' Mary said, 'No, I don't want to go. If he wants me he'll have to come and get me himself.'"

"John left," Mary says, "and I stayed in the car. I was in the front seat, not the driver's seat, but the other."

Back down in the wash, John found Alleen lying on the ground, on her back. "Her face and head were covered with blood," John says. "Smitty's hands were bloody . . . and the front of his shirt. He said, 'Where's Mary?' I said, 'She said for you to come and get her.' "

Mary was still waiting at the car. "Smitty came up to the car," she says. "He was talking but I never said anything. He was breathing real hard—he seemed excited. . . . He got in the car and said, 'We killed her.' He said, 'I love you very much,' and he kissed me and he went back of the car and got the shovel. . . . The next morning there was blood on my blouse where he touched me, on my shoulder."

At the car, Mary says Smitty told her that John had struck Alleen with a rock. "And he said, 'She took off running,' and John chased her and hit her again. He said John tried to have relations with her but he couldn't."

Mary got out of the car and walked back down to the wash with Smitty. Alleen was on the ground, "a couple of yards from where John was just standing there. . . . She just had the bathing suit on. The curlers were off and she was all messed up . . . blood on her face and her head." Mary noticed no signs of movement or breathing from Alleen that might indicate she was still alive.

Smitty told John to start digging, and handed him the shovel.

John started digging. Smitty said, "Come on . . . we've got to bury her." Smitty began to dig with his hands. He said to John, "Give Mary the shovel."

Mary says, "They told me to start digging, so I dug." John and Smitty continued digging with their hands. "Smitty told me to take her feet and he took her arms and put her in the hole. John was holding her somewhere on the side."

The three placed the body into the hole. John remembers that he took the shift from the ground and put it in the hole while Smitty started shoveling dirt in over the body. Mary then relieved Smitty with the shoveling while he and John gathered up the haircurlers from around the area, "put them in a pile," Mary says, "and took and threw some sand over them."

John helped Mary fill up the hole. "Better leave the shovel," Smitty said. He then took off his bloodstained shirt and buried that along with the shovel. "We went back up the slope to the car," Mary says. "They wiped the car of fingerprints . . . the back seat . . . then they took me home."

On the way home, Mary remembers, "Smitty wanted us to stick to the same story that John had a date with her that night and when we went over to pick her up she wasn't home, so we took John home and then the two of us went out."

◆

When Norma Rowe returned from work early that
morning, she went to bed thinking all her children
were in school and didn't wake up until her two boys
returned that afternoon. It occurred to her then that
Alleen should have been home from school before her
brothers, since her classes at Palo Verde let out earlier.
Clint, Norma's oldest son, said that he hadn't seen
Alleen but suggested she'd remained after school for
something.

Norma went about her household chores and began
to notice that things were not as they usually were.
Alleen had left her bed unmade—that was unusual. In
her room she saw the school books on the table where
she remembered seeing them the night before, and
Alleen's purse was still there. Sitting on the edge of
Alleen's bed, she checked the money and personal
things Alleen always took with her. Looking around
uneasily, Norma saw that the room had not changed
since she'd left for work. Something seemed wrong to
Norma.

She examined her daughter's closet and found nothing missing except the black bathing suit Alleen had
been wearing. Then Norma telephoned Palo Verde. The
administrative office informed her that Alleen had not
attended any of her classes.

Hanging up, she sat stunned for several moments,
wondering what she should do. She placed calls to a
number of people who might possibly know where
Alleen was. No one had any idea where Alleen might
have gone or if anything had happened to her. Then

Norma remembered that the night before Alleen had phoned the university student she had been going with, but had been unable to reach him. Norma spoke to the boy at length but he had no knowledge of Alleen's whereabouts.

By now it was dark. Norma Rowe faced the fact that her daughter was really missing. Reluctantly, she telephoned the police department.

The evening before, six criminals had escaped from the Pima County Jail felony tank. During the night sheriff's officers and police search parties had apprehended five, but the sixth and most desperate criminal had eluded the patrols until late that morning. The urgency had slackened at police headquarters by the time an officer received Norma Rowe's call.

"Girls disappear for a while after disagreements with their parents," he told Mrs. Rowe, "some have a boy friend the parents don't take a liking to and there's other reasons why juveniles take off, but usually they return home as soon as they're hungry." The officer said, "This happens more often than——"

"You're wrong," Norma said. "This is not the case with my daughter, Alleen." She reported the reasons for her apprehension: the unmade bed, the purse and books untouched, an above-average student absent from an entire day of school. None of Alleen's clothes were missing, she told the officer, she'd taken no money, and all she'd been wearing was a bathing suit.

"Only a bathing suit?" the officer said, interested, but he repeated his reassurances. Mrs. Rowe was quick to deny that this particular case had anything to do with boy friends, elopements, disagreements with parents.

She said her daughter had never left home before and she knew something terrible had happened to her. She reported that Alleen's boy friend at the university said that he hadn't seen her. Then she mentioned the names of other friends of her daughter, people she didn't approve of.

Fears for her daughter's safety had been building in her all day. After a pause she revealed to the officer what he later told a fellow policeman was one of the most ridiculous and weird stories he'd ever heard from a mother.

She said Alleen had reported to her that some kind of sex club, involving young boys and girls from Palo Verde and other schools, was in operation, engaging in perverse sexual conduct, drugs, liquor, and organized prostitution. Alleen had told her, Norma said, that the leaders of the group had tried to get her into the club but her daughter had repeatedly refused to have anything to do with them. Now, Norma feared, this group had tried to force Alleen into their terrible activities, Alleen had again refused, and the leaders had done something to keep Alleen quiet.

The police would investigate, the officer said, and he asked Norma to contact them immediately as soon as she received any word from her daughter. Mrs. Rowe replied that she was afraid she would never hear from her daughter again.

Discussing the situation with his fellow officer, the policeman who had taken the call wondered whether such a thing could actually exist at one of Tucson's better high schools.

"It might just be," the fellow officer said, "that some of these women might not know their daughter's ways like they might think they do."

An investigation failed to disclose any evidence to support Norma Rowe's suspicions. It failed, in fact, to reveal anything in the Rowe neighborhood that was out of the ordinary except the girl's disappearance. Norma rechecked her daughter's wardrobe and only one other piece of clothing was missing, a yellow checked shift with a lace hem. Nothing in the house suggested that Alleen had been removed from the premises by force; her two brothers, asleep at the time of her disappearance, would have heard something had the girl been forced from the house. No indication of a struggle of any kind existed. But where could she have gone, they wondered, in nothing but a bathing suit and a yellow shift?

During the days that followed, Norma kept after the police. She carefully drafted a list of people she suspected. With nothing else to go on, the police questioned those on the list, but none of them provided any information regarding Alleen. The names included Mary French, who was questioned eight or nine times the first day, and John Saunders and Charles Schmid.

On that first day, Mary recalls that Smitty called her about every half hour, "Maybe ten times or more. He wanted to know if the police had been over to question me and he said that they would ask him to take a lie-detector test." At 5:30 that evening, "Smitty came over to my house. He stayed a short time and then went home. . . . He returned about eight o'clock with John Saunders." Mary says they drove out to River Road and "up some dirt path and parked there."

Then, "Smitty made us both repeat the story that we were going to tell the police so that we would all have it straight." It was about ten or ten-thirty when he drove Mary home.

A week after Alleen's disappearance, Norma Rowe's ex-husband telephoned from Texas to relate a dream he'd had, "a nightmare," in which his daughter was murdered in the desert.

Norma was convinced that the dream was in fact what had happened. She repeated it to the police, who said they were interested in more factual evidence. Despite Norma's constant suggestions, the police had nothing to go on, no starting point from which a proper investigation could proceed.

Detective Sergeant Robert Wilhelm, in charge of Juvenile Detail, conferred with Tucson Police Chief Bernard Garmire, but had little to tell him. Working under Wilhelm, several other detectives questioned and requestioned a number of people who knew Alleen, but none of the leads checked out.

Then, on July 1st, one month after Alleen's disappearance, the police made a public announcement that the investigation had intensified and would continue. Actually, however, very little had happened aside from routine procedure.

Meanwhile Mrs. Rowe conferred with reporters, private detectives, and anyone who expressed even a remote interest in the search for her daughter. A salesman calling on her would be informed of the facts, of the indifference of the police, and would be enlisted as a source of possible information.

Alleen's school acquaintances were requestioned, as were Mary French, John Saunders, and Charles Schmid. Nobody gave any information. The adolescents were called in again and again until their parents and later their family lawyers began to complain. Injunctions were obtained prohibiting the police from further interrogations of the children. One lawyer stated, "These kids have no information and are being badgered by the police to cover up for their own lack of information about the missing girl."

Of course, there were a number of unconfirmed reports. Alleen had been seen down in Nogales, across the street on Stone Avenue, and in a number of southwestern cities. The police kept trying, but after a while they began to lose interest. Alleen's Palo Verde class moved into its junior year; there was still some gossip at school as to what had happened to her, but there were a lot of other things to talk about.

In March 1965, Norma Rowe went to Phoenix to discuss the case with the state's Attorney General and demand results. She said the Tucson police were apathetic and that *something* had to be done. Dissatisfied with the reassurances of the Attorney General's office, she then went to the head of the Federal Bureau of Investigation in Arizona. He didn't know very much about the case. Calling in reporters, she told them she was meeting with the U.S. Attorney's office in Tucson and that she had hired her own lawyer and would continue to pursue the issue "until they find my daughter one way or the other."

In the first week in March, Norma met again with the press. Her spirits sagging, she told them, "The police think she is simply a runaway. I'm sure she is dead—she's lost forever."

A week later Clint Rowe, age fourteen, answered the telephone and heard the voice of an anonymous caller who sounded like an old woman. The caller said she was bothered by what appeared to be "a grave near the end of the greens." She went on to tell Clint that "in the past there has been some really rough groups of kids out there, drinking and having wild parties."

The same anonymous caller talked to police and was more specific. She told them of seeing a grave near the golf course at Rolling Hills Estates and suggested that it could very well conceal the body of a young girl.

On Saturday morning the police, led by Sergeant Wilhelm, walked through the area the caller had indicated. They could not find the grave in question or anything even resembling a grave, although they searched not only "the end of the greens" but the entire course and surrounding area. Later, Mrs. Rowe conducted her own search of the golf course, without obtaining any results. But the news of the search stirred up more calls, leads, and contradictory hints as to the girl's whereabouts, none of them useful. More missing-persons bulletins were mimeographed and sent to law-enforcement agencies, where they were piled on top of fliers in similar cases, all of them describing girls who seemed to have vanished into the air.

Looking anywhere for an answer, Norma Rowe consulted a New Jersey psychic. The oracle proved cryptic, and at her request Norma sent the woman an item belonging to Alleen, to be used as an inductor; the idea was for the woman to hold the inductor in her hands and through it receive vibrations which would clarify the mental picture. Nothing happened.

Alleen's former classmates finished their junior year and left Palo Verde for summer vacations. Nothing had come of the official inquiry. The missing-persons bulletin on Alleen Rowe was buried under a pile of more recent cases.

◆

During the month of May 1964 (the month Alleen Rowe vanished), Paul Graff married the girl he had been living with and moved away from Smitty and his friends. A few weeks later Mary French left Tucson temporarily and Smitty drove his motorcycle to Phoenix to take a physical for the army.

Smitty wanted no part of the service. "I resisted for

two basic reasons," he says, "one being the regimentation and conformity, and the other that I didn't particularly relish the idea of shooting somebody to satisfy the whim of some idiot." When he filled out the forms, he listed himself as a conscientious objector, but the army didn't accept this as reason for deferrment since Smitty had stated no religious preference. "Fortunately," he says, "my heart had an irregular beat—probably rock 'n' roll—and my blood pressure was so low I was listed officially as 1-Y. . . . I burned up the highway on the way back from Phoenix."

Although Smitty was once again receiving an allowance of $300 a month, Katharine and Charles Schmid, Sr.'s, luxurious new hospital had gone into receivership, and the Schmids were entering litigation.

Lawyer John Price, acting on the Schmids' behalf, had obtained an injunction prohibiting the police from requestioning Smitty in the Alleen Rowe disappearance. Following that, John Saunders left Tucson to join the Navy, and now Richie Bruns was seeing Smitty almost every day. "It was like we were brothers," Richie says.

According to Smitty, "It was like Richie wanted to tell me everything. I couldn't figure it out. I told him I wasn't his father confessor and didn't have to hear the sordid details of his life story, but he'd say, 'Yes, I have to. You've got to know. We're friends, aren't we?' But confessing things to me didn't seem to stop him from continuing to do them, the things he did, that he couldn't stop doing."

But it didn't matter to Smitty as he had stories of

his own to tell. Richie says that Smitty habitually told him "stories about what a terrible man he was," and, encouraged by Smitty's confidence, Richie in turn would divulge his secrets, many of them fictional. Once he told Smitty that he'd hitched a ride on a freight train and found an old hobo in a car.

"I pushed this old bum out of the car," Richie said, ". . . I watched him fall and I think he broke his back or something. He made a weird noise hitting the ground."

Smitty wanted to know if, in Richie's opinion, the hobo had turned to a skeleton. Richie said, "Yeah, if he's dead . . . if no one found him. I really believe I killed him."

During the early summer, Richie recalls, Smitty had wanted to order a pair of piranha fish from South America. They could be bred in a big jar, kept warm, then dumped into Sabino Lake. "All the kids with skinned knees," Richie had said, "like those Band-Aid commercials on television."

One night after cruising the teen-age hangout, they wound up at Johnnie's Drive-In on Stone Avenue with "nowhere to go and nothing to do." Smitty suggested they drive to San Diego.

Richie agreed and took over the driving. "I was speeding," Richie says, "and drunk too. I kept banging against the sides of the hills and every time I'd hit a dip in the road, Smitty would bounce around in the back seat where he was sleeping. Once I hit a bend so hard it tossed him off the seat and on the floor. . . .

He just got back up and tried to make himself comfortable. He was using my jacket as a pillow."

They checked into a cheap hotel in San Diego and cruised the beaches the following day. "There were all these sailors running around the place and Smitty said we might run into John Saunders. Later, Smitty suggested we catch a couple of girls, rape them, and murder them."

That night in San Diego, "We prowled around the beaches, even underneath the piers and along those water-front hotdog stands . . . hunting for victims.

"But it was getting cold and my jacket was back at the hotel. Smitty kept on walking around the beaches and I walked back to the hotel. When I got back in the room I jacked-off . . . it relieved the tension and then I got my jacket." Richie wanted to return to Tucson. He says, "Smitty was still prowling the beach like a wolf and I said 'Come on, man, come on.' "

In July 1964 Smitty noticed a sixteen-year-old blonde at Himmel Park Swimming Pool off Speedway. She was wearing a polka-dot bathing suit, sandals, and her shoulder-length yellow hair waved from side to side as she ran along the edge of the pool. Her name was Gretchen Fritz. She seemed a little nervous, jumpy, and there was something about her, a stray-cat look in her eyes, that made Smitty think of her as being "like a wreck looking for it to happen."

He pointed the "skinny blonde" out to Richie, who then found out the names of the boys Gretchen had been going with. Smitty saw that she was driving a new red-and-white Le Mans and he flirted with her at the pool. When she left, he followed her home, staying well behind so that she wouldn't notice him.

From what he could see of her house behind the adobe wall that enclosed the property, it seemed almost like a mansion. She lived on East Elm, one of the most fashionable streets in Tucson.

Gretchen's father, Dr. James Fritz, was one of the leading heart and chest specialists in the Southwest, a board member of the Union Bank, and his wife, Nancy, was socially prominent. They attended all the best parties in Tucson. Gretchen had two older sisters, both married, one younger brother, and a younger sister, Wendy, still in junior high school.

But Gretchen was different from the other members of her family. She didn't fit in at the exclusive private school her parents sent her to; she was a nonconformist with eccentric ideas: she told a classmate she scorned boys and admired prostitutes "who get money for what most boys expect to get free." One teacher regarded Gretchen as a "troublemaker, and the child is a psychopathic liar."

Her contemporaries considered her spoiled: "I guess beyond repair," one girl said, and added that she was almost "psychotically jealous." Gretchen had a bad reputation among teen-agers as an "easy put-out," and when asked about such matters Gretchen seemed pleased and offered a wry smile. "They're just jealous," she'd say.

Gretchen was constantly cutting classes to cruise Speedway and was suspected of various juvenile crimes. In the summer of her senior year she was in serious trouble over the attempted holdup of a liquor store. The headmaster of the school requested that she not return and recommended psychiatric treatment.

"Gretchen was all right with the girls," a friend recalls, "but the minute a boy was there she'd change— bang, like that, a Jekyll-Hyde sort of thing."

Several days after he had noticed Gretchen at the pool, Smitty went into the kitchen at Craycroft Center and loaded an assortment of pots and pans into a cardboard box. Then he set out for East Elm.

The box was clumsy but he juggled it up to Gretchen's house. Gretchen answered the door and Smitty told her he was selling pots and pans. She seemed reluctant to let him in. But when she recognized him from the swimming pool she said it would be okay. Smitty immediately launched into a spiel on pots and pans and unloaded the cardboard box.

"But they all look like they've been used," Gretchen said. Smitty then explained that these were samples, and tried to get them back into the box. Gretchen watched him curiously and said she would buy them all.

"These particular ones are not for sale," Smitty said. "They're my samples. . . ."

"But I want these," Gretchen insisted. Smitty was just as insistent that he couldn't sell his samples. If he did, he'd get fired, he said. Gretchen didn't believe him; then Smitty confessed that he wasn't a salesman at all.

"I dreamed it all up to meet you," he said. "I couldn't just come here and knock on your door; I really and truly didn't want to be that brash. It would be like I was trying to pick you up."

Gretchen started to laugh, and then suddenly she was crying. Smitty didn't understand it. She hurried from the room, only to return moments later and ask if he cared for a cocktail. Her mercurial moods aroused a different interest in him. He felt foolish about the pots and pans, and accepted.

Gretchen brought two drinks to the sofa and she and Smitty sat and talked. She said no one had ever cared enough before to dream up something that stupid, and added that he'd be surprised at some of the "lines" she'd heard. "If you want," she said, "we can meet at Sabino tomorrow. . . ."

Richie Bruns went with Smitty to Sabino Canyon the following day. Richie says, "Gretchen had two of her scummy girls friends with her. This one fat pig kept trying to nestle up close to me. Smitty kept telling her about 'Richie,' he wanted her to go with me so we could double on the way back.

"I had my quart of beer and was content to sit on the rock and enjoy my beer, watch the water, you know. This pig, you could just see oil and grime all over her. And she was sweating."

Richie insulted the girl and Gretchen "blew her

mind. She sort of fell in the water, then Smitty pushed her the rest of the way in with all her clothes on."

Recalling that day, Richie says, "I believe my insulting her pig friend is the reason Gretchen and I disliked one another from the start. It only got progressively worse."

On his first date with Gretchen, Smitty remembers, "She had too much to drink, although she handled it as though it was an everyday occurrence with her. She began to tell me she was pregnant, the guy had left her and she said her parents didn't love her. She said she hated her family and had tried to run away several times. Last time she'd been sent to a private school. Once she'd tried to rob the liquor store with some friends (the ones that had been at Sabino with her).

"She told me she was afraid of her parents and her brother-in-law had something to do with the Mafia. The more she spoke about her problems, guys leaving her, family disagreements, the more I felt myself feeling something for her. It was like 'Here we go again.'"

Richie says, "Smitty screwed her in short order, but she cried when he took off her bra, because nothing was there."

When it was over, Smitty recalls, ". . . she jerked back and said, 'Now that you've got what you want you'll leave just like the rest, because I know you're no different than them.' I said, 'What do you know about me?' I couldn't hurt her, not then, and I said I wasn't like the rest. 'I probably love you,' I told her.

"As soon as some time had passed and we were going

around together, being seen at Johnnie's almost every night for a while, the word got around and I started to receive various stories about Gretchen. . . . I didn't believe them, but . . ."

Richie had talked to a number of boys Gretchen had gone with, and their advice to Smitty was to keep away from her. Even one of Gretchen's friends warned him: "She'll get you in one hell of a mess and she won't care. She does things like the world belongs to her."

Once she ran out of gas on Speedway and, with the help of a girl friend, siphoned gas from a car at the curb. The police caught them and she was in trouble again.

One boy told Smitty, "Gretchen is *dangerous,* just like it says on a box of *dynamite.*"

But Smitty became increasingly involved with Gretchen Fritz. "Gretchen's father caught me naked at her house once but he didn't make me stop seeing her. I used to slip in through her window at night; we'd make love while her parents were asleep in another part of the house. Her mother saw footprints outside Gretchen's window and discovered what was happening. She didn't know I was having sex with Gretchen but she suspected."

A friend sums up Gretchen's relationship with Smitty: "She was always lonely and looking for someone to love her. At times she didn't even care who it was. Smitty gave her what she wanted but she was afraid of losing him. She knew he was going out with other girls, like Mary French for one, and when she'd find out they would quarrel. I remember one night they were at a show and started arguing about something. Smitty had to hit her several times to stop her hysterics. She cried a lot but never told me what they'd fought about. Then, five minutes later, they were holding each other. . . . It wasn't easy to get to know Gretchen."

After a while Smitty considered breaking off with Gretchen. He didn't want to leave her but his friends told him it would be the best thing.

One of them suggested an "out" for Smitty by putting her in the wrong. The idea, according to Smitty, was "for me to catch her with another guy, thus giving me an excuse. So Richie, Johnny, and I got this kid, Charles Stenz, to have her meet him at the park, the plan being that I'd come out of the bushes, act angry, then break up with her. Richie would be hiding in the bushes and be there as a witness. Everything went according to plan. . . . Gretchen turned up . . ."

The way Richie remembers what followed: "Smitty slapped her. . . . But then Gretchen told him that Charles Stenz, to bait her into coming, had told her that he had something he wanted to tell her about Smitty, and so she had come not just for the sake of going out, and Smitty made up with her."

Smitty says, "I tried to break up with her but couldn't manage it . . . and once before when I'd tried to break up with her she'd gotten drunk and was arrested for reckless driving, going on the wrong side of Speedway against the traffic. They put her on probation."

Complicating Smitty's relation with Gretchen was an apparent rivalry between Gretchen and Richie. "I never really understood why," Smitty says, "but she made life miserable for him in general." Gretchen said the reason she didn't care for Richie was that she feared he would involve Smitty in some serious trouble. Richie had been to a reformatory and thus represented a bad influence on Smitty. Richie also had the habit of confessing some actual and fictional misdeeds to Smitty, which alarmed Gretchen.

Smitty says, "I told her that Richie kept telling me about his activities, saying he had to even though it was none of my business, and Gretchen said, 'He wants you to know as much as he does, so you'll both be the same.' I'd say she was wrong."

Art Meyers had a more dispassionate view of the situation. "Bruns and Smitty were always together—inseparable. But Richie didn't like Gretchen at all, he told me he despised her. He had no specific reason. I didn't like her either. Gretchen thought she was pretty cool. She thought she was too hot, if you know what I mean."

Smitty felt that Richie had trouble dating girls. "From the time I knew him he went out with only four girls on his own and they all eventually dropped him. Some of them told me he was either on pills, drunk, or would try to rape them in some way. He used to bring some slob to the house on Woodland and once some girls we picked up at the drive-in. I had a hard time with Gretchen because she found out all about the ones we picked up at the A-1 Drive-In, and she seemed to know all the details."

Smitty says that he tried to arrange dates for Richie. "But they all disliked him or wouldn't go out with him. I wasn't really aware of it at the time but Gretchen was blackballing him at school with all the other girls. At one party he and Gretchen got into a serious fight. . . . I didn't exactly understand what he was talking about . . . until I learned that he'd been black-balled."

One night Richie was drunk and got into trouble on his own. Smitty recalls, "Gretchen really enjoyed finding out about it. She made it seem as though it was a lesson, and I should learn from it. I couldn't appreciate her view, as Richie and I had parties, booze, and girls and a lot of kicks. I pretended to take it seriously, only trying to keep Gretchen in place and thinking that I was totally true to her and had nothing to do with anyone else.

"It required ingenuity on my part; Gretchen was hardly a fool. I thought that being engaged to her, Mary French and Darlene Kirk would satisfy me but even then I wanted more.

"I even seriously thought of bigamy—if somewhere along the line I could meet two relatively wealthy girls, I'd marry them both under aliases and live off them comfortably. I'd use the guitar playing as an excuse to be gone for long periods of time, while I lived with one, then the other. I used to laugh when I thought of the predicaments I'd be in if the record I planned to cut turned out successfully.

"Now how could I sensibly explain that I did go with three girls at once and I did give them rings and it was necessary for me to fabricate certain stories so as not to be discovered?

"Gretchen demanded my fidelity, or fidelity on the part of anyone she went with, but as soon as my back was turned she was running around herself. The only thing I had in my favor was that she wasn't as cool about it as I was."

◆

Darlene Kirk, a thin, brown-haired sixteen-year-old daughter of a Tucson postman, was one of Smitty's steadies at the time, one of the girls he proposed marriage to. Smitty had asked Darlene to baby-sit and give him the money she earned so he could further his rock 'n' roll career. Darlene was a Presley fan. Richie says, "She had Elvis pictures stuck to her mirror and life-sized ones all over the windows." Although she could appreciate Smitty's emulation of her idol, she wasn't enthusiastic about investing in his career.

According to Bruns, Smitty hoped to get money by becoming engaged to her. "He bought her a $3 engagement ring and told her, 'Cutting a record will cost money,' as he slipped the ring on her finger. 'Before we can get married,' Smitty told her, 'I'll need a lot of money.' " When Darlene didn't contribute, Smitty told her he had other things to do.

"Darlene was moping around the school," Richie recalls, "and asking, 'Why won't Smitty call me?' " She used to give Richie messages to pass on to Smitty, and "whenever she did see Smitty, she always wore black stockings because Smitty had told her to." Finally, after some tearful scenes, she gave Richie the engagement ring to return to Smitty. Richie said he couldn't do that, and then considered dating her himself. "Smitty," he rationalized, "couldn't care less about her or the other girls."

After a couple of dates, Richie felt that Darlene could hold her liquor. He prized himself on being a seasoned drinker, and especially detested Gretchen's "inability at holding liquor . . . she was notorious for it. She would get totally out of her head on one can of beer, and at a party for El Rancho stores, where Paul was working, Gretchen barfed all over the tables. It was disgusting."

Later, Bruns and Gretchen were involved in an incident that confirmed their mutual dislike. Richie had acquired a white 1950 Cadillac convertible, and one night he says, "I was with a girl named Mimi and we were pulling out of Johnnie's on Speedway and Craycroft and Smitty was coming down the street on the other side and had Gretchen with him and he saw me going out and he honked.

"I pulled over and he went through Johnnie's and

came back over. . . . He asked me who the girl was, what her name was, and Gretchen whispered in his ear that she looked like a whore, and Mimi heard it, so, after we left and were driving around, Mimi decided she wanted to fight Gretchen or make her take it back.

"I took Mimi over to Smitty's and I told Smitty that she wanted to fight Gretchen. And Smitty said, 'That sounds like a pretty good idea.' He said that to me, 'This is what she needs.' We decided to get a double date and go out to the show and give Mimi a chance to fight Gretchen. So I went home and later that night he called me up and said he talked to Gretchen, but Gretchen was expecting trouble and she made him promise that when any trouble started Smitty would make both of us get out and walk home. He said, 'What we'll do, is go get the BB gun over at Paul's, take the BB's out and everything, and when she makes me leave the car you pull the gun on me and in that way it won't make me look so bad and I won't have to make you walk home.' "

Richie got the BB gun from Paul and later that night at a drive-in movie, Richie says, "Mimi asked Gretchen why she called her a whore. Gretchen denied that she called her a whore and Mimi said, 'Why, I heard you.' Gretchen said, 'You are imagining things, seeing something.' Mimi kept taking her cigarette and flicking it on Gretchen's hair and so kept giving her a hard time. But Gretchen wouldn't get out of the car and fight, and finally she turned to Smitty and said, 'All right, make him get out.'

"Smitty turned around and winked at me and I pulled the gun on him and I said, 'Uh-uh, I ain't going nowhere.'" Mimi and Gretchen continued to bicker and they decided to leave the drive-in. Richie told Smitty to keep driving and at one point left the car and ditched the gun in the desert. "Finally, I went home and Smitty came over and picked me up and we got the gun and took it back to Paul's."

Days later, everyone was talking about how Richie pulled a gun at the drive-in.

According to Richie, Smitty was jealous of anyone even mildly interested in Gretchen. He developed several interesting ploys to keep her out of the reach of prospective rivals. He involved Bruns in a campaign of writing anonymous letters to Gretchen's parents, containing such questions as: "Where was your darling daughter when you were having dinner last night? She was down at Johnnie's seeing Smitty." Smitty had Bruns write these on his typewriter, because, he claimed, Gretchen's mother knew his handwriting. The idea was to have Gretchen's parents keep a closer eye on her so that she'd have less chance to see other boys. Smitty then dictated letters concerning Gretchen and VD to the health department, letters Richie would type and mail for Smitty.

Then Smitty told Gretchen that Richie was behind the letters, and knew everything about her. According to Richie, Smitty said to Gretchen: "Richie has all this stuff over your head and he's blackmailing me with you—that if I stop hanging around with him, stop loaning him money and that, he's going to the police with all he knows about you and you'll be sent to Good Shepherd."

As this time, Richie and Smitty were still competing with each other in the stories they told about themselves. They had carried it a step further, according to Richie, by planning crimes—assaults, mayhem, and even murder together.

One night at Smitty's they were talking about Gretchen, about Darlene, and then about how they hated a girl named Mary Tyler. Richie recalls, "Smitty suggested, 'Let's go get her.' He said, 'I'll take care of the old man and old lady, and you take care of Mary and her brother.'" Another boy actually drove them over to the house, and while Smitty waited in the car, Richie scaled a wall and made his way to the rear of the house. The plan was for Richie to gain entrance for Smitty. Richie attempted to open the rear door but it was dead-bolted.

"I stood there for a minute," Richie remembers, "and thought about the time we went to San Diego. Then I just faked the rest of it." When he returned to the car he told Smitty "someone's walking around in there. Let's get out of here."

It was not long thereafter that Smitty related to Richie what had actually happened to Alleen Rowe. John Saunders had been discharged from the Navy and was accompanying Richie, Smitty, and another boy named Rick on a hunting trip through the Golf Links area. "Smitty and John went down into the wash to scare up some rabbits," Richie recalls, "and they were gone approximately half an hour."

Later, "at the golf place, parked at the corner of Desert and 15th . . . Smitty referred back to our previous conversations, when he told me that he had been questioned in the case after the girl disappeared, and his lawyer had got an injunction against the police and they couldn't talk to him about it, he was bragging about that, but he told me at this time that he did kill Alleen Rowe, and that when they'd left the car on the hunting trip they didn't go down to scare up jackrabbits but went down to the grave and that he stuck a stick in the ground to see how she smelled after she had been there so long. . . .

"He said an animal had burrowed itself into where the grave was and had been eating the body."

Bruns did not give much further thought to Smitty's story. The following week, however, while waiting in Smitty's car which he was using to pick up Darlene Kirk at Rincon, Richie mentioned to a couple of kids that Smitty was supposed to have murdered the Rowe girl. Richie says, "it was just conversation, like what's new."

One night Richie was drinking beer with Smitty and Saunders at the Hi-Ho. "John had been caught shoplifting," Richie recalls, "and there was something about an assault charge against him." John and Smitty were talking and Richie was concentrating on his beer when the subject of the Rowe girl came up.

Richie remembers John asking Smitty: "Did you ever burn those clothes?"

"What clothes?" Smitty asked.

John said, "Oh—*hers*—you know."

Smitty looked at him and shook his head, and said, "Wow, what's the matter with you? She wasn't even wearing any clothes."

The next afternoon, sitting in Johnnie's Drive-in, Smitty told Richie the details of the Rowe killing. Richie says, "He told me that Mary French had gotten Alleen out of the house and that they drove out there and Smitty and Saunders took Alleen down into the wash there and they made her take off her bathing suit, and that both of them had sexual relations with her and then they made her put back on her bathing suit.

"First of all he tried to strangle her, but she wouldn't strangle—she kept doing something with her chin, so he picked up a rock and bashed it over her head and then he went back to the car and got a shovel and buried her on the side of the hill underneath a tree and he said that if Mary French ever knew he had relations with her she would probably kill him."

In September, while Paul was staying at Smitty's house for a week, Smitty also told Paul about the murder. Paul didn't believe Smitty. "He told me they buried her in the desert," Paul says. "He asked me to go out there and see the grave, almost in a joking manner. I didn't go."

Several days after Paul left, Richie tried without success to call Smitty. He found him at the Ranch Restaurant after spotting the Falcon in the parking lot.

Richie said to Smitty: "I called you all day yesterday and there was no answer. What's the deal?"

Smitty replied, "I fixed the phone so it won't ring. I can turn it back on and it'll ring when I want it to."

"What did you do that for?" Richie asked.

"Gretchen's been calling night and day," Smitty said. "I know if the damn thing rings I'll pick it up."

Richie began to think. "Nobody bugged the Smitty I knew," he says. "Nobody bothered the Smitty I knew. So I asked him why he was doing all this stuff for Gretchen. He was acting like a little kid.

"He told me he'd taken her out there and showed her Alleen Rowe, and she was holding that over his head, if he didn't do exactly what she said.

"He took her out there to show her what sort of guy he was, to see if she still loved him. He's that way, he wants to find out if people care, if anyone cares. He couldn't be normal. But girls ate on him."

Gretchen was "blackmailing" Smitty and it was beginning to "get under his skin." He discussed with Richie ways of hurting Gretchen. "He knew when her parents would go out, which was quite often. She would be home alone at night. What he wanted me to do was—he would call to Gretchen when her parents were gone, he would get on the phone, and Gretchen would naturally ask if I was there and he would say, 'Yeah,' and he would want people to verify it at his folks' hospital there that were watching. While he was talking on the phone, I was to go and ring Gretchen's doorbell and when she would open the door I was to throw acid in her face."

But Smitty's feelings about Gretchen were still ambivalent. Richie says, "If he fucked up Gretchen, nobody would want her, but he said, 'If I really fucked her up, then maybe I wouldn't want her either.' It was good logic."

◆

In October 1964, Katharine and Charles Schmid, Sr., declared bankruptcy. Katharine's luxurious Craycroft Center had gone into receivership and the Schmids estimated their loss at over $300,000. They returned to Hillcrest on East Adams, where Smitty took over the small one-bedroom house next door to the Schmids' home.

Smitty painted the bedroom windows and two glass doors that opened to the back yard, flat black. He laid a green satin spread over the bed, installed his stereo next to it, and began to entertain his friends. But Richie felt that he was losing contact with Smitty.

"We were known on the east side," Richie says, "especially after that incident with the gun at the drive-in.

"After Smitty moved on Adams, he began hanging around with some south-side people." Richie resented Smitty having left the "east-side bunch," for Richie didn't know anyone from the south side. "Smitty uses people, except me and Paul.

"I used Smitty's car, his credit cards, I even used Smitty's credit cards to put gas in my car. Outside of Paul and myself he used everyone, especially on East Adams, and all they did was sit around and listen on some old rusty record player."

One of Smitty's friends from the south side was a sixteen-year-old girl named Irma Jean Kolt. She'd dropped out of Pueblo High School after being absent twenty-seven days the first three months of her sophomore year. Irma Jean was also the mother of an infant whose father had fled Tucson on receiving news of his coming paternity. In the summer of 1965 she was unemployed and living with her parents.

According to Smitty, "Irma Jean was a pretty screwed-up kid; her father had one arm missing and was always out of work while her mother, an alcoholic, had been in and out of mental hygiene clinics for years, but fun at times if she was loaded.

"I'd lost my license over a traffic ticket and my car had been impounded. So, in Irma Jean's mom's car, with Mrs. Kolt driving, somewhere about July 15th, we headed down to Nogales along with Shirley and Kitty Bates, two teen-age sisters that didn't do much except goof around Speedway."

They had lunch across the border, a few drinks, and

did some shopping. Returning to Tucson they came across a stalled car whose driver was waving to the passing cars. His name was Bill Morgen and he was out of gas. His wife was slumped in the front seat.

"Our car is so damn crowded we can hardly move," Smitty recalls, "so the girls say sorry, with all the packages we don't have room to take you into town for gas. So we leave. Except that I started spouting off how rotten it is just to leave them there. We go back and give them a ride twenty-five miles into town for gas and then return them.

"When they tell me their hard-luck story, down and out, no place to go, broke flat, I offer them my house and food, free, until they can get on their feet." Gassed up, the Bates' car followed Smitty back to Tucson. "We drop them off at my house, then go to the Kolts' house, where Irma Jean leaves her mom, and the three girls take me home.

"They came in for a while, while the Morgens were there and then, on their way out, Irma Jean was adjusting her blouse when Gretchen pulls up and sees Irma Jean doing this; naturally, she gets the wrong idea. Furious, Gretchen chased me around the house and I climbed a tree in the back yard. She tried to climb up after me but she couldn't, so she threw rocks instead, then raced off to find Irma Jean and the other girls somewhere up Speedway. They all stopped, I learned later, and one thing led to another. After the insults they talked, Irma Jean and Shirley told Gretchen about me messing around with other girls, and told her the name of one that I was engaged to. Gretchen blew her mind."

Smitty had to do something immediately to cool things with Gretchen. "I quickly told them (the girls) a fantastic story, to the effect that Gretchen had a diary that said I'd killed some guy because he had run over my girl friend and left, that I'd taken him out to the desert, shot him, and then buried him. I decided on something drastic because it would tie in with part two of my plan—the Blackmail Bit. I fabricated a story that Gretchen knew I was messing around and she would have me arrested by turning the diary over to the police. Irma Jean and Shirley agreed to help, to get me back on good terms with Gretchen. I told them to tell Gretchen I wasn't messing around and that they had just tried to make her jealous, which they knew they could.

"The plan got more involved when I even told Irma Jean's mother that Gretchen had something on me, because I knew that Gretchen would believe *her* if she confirmed that I wasn't messing around with other girls. I laughed to myself at the cleverness, the way I'd smoothed things over.

"Bill Morgen and his wife Doris were there in my house and didn't seem to have any intentions of leaving." It occurred to Smitty that the Morgens might talk to Gretchen, "and unknowingly tell her, if she asked, what I did with other girls." So Smitty told the Morgens the same story he'd told the Kolts and the Bates sisters. "In fact I hinted to several people that

Gretchen was blackmailing me; this of course allowed me greater freedom in my choice of girls and enabled me to keep Gretchen cool at the same time. All I did was simply insert a few key words and they took the blackmail bit from there. I naturally figured if it worked so good before, it would again and it did, at the time."

While all this was going on, Smitty was becoming more involved with his house guests. "Bill Morgen showed no concern or enthusiasm about looking for work. . . . I wondered exactly what sort of trade Bill might have. He told me he was an upholsterer and that he'd lost his business.

"It was another hard-luck story, but the prospect of an upholstery business sounded interesting to me. My mom was having trouble at the time with the bankruptcy, so I couldn't get the extra money from her. It was sort of up to me. I offered to hock all my guitars and equipment and use whatever money I had on the side to set us up in business.

"One night the Morgens had a big fight and Doris called the police and had her husband arrested for being drunk. She kept screaming out in the street even after the cops had taken him to jail. And she blamed me for his drinking. My mother asked them to leave, but the next day it was discussed and I hocked the rest of my equipment to start again.

"No sooner had we managed to establish the upholstery shop at my house than Irma Jean's father arrived looking for work, so we took him in as a partner. I felt sorry for him, having only one arm, and the other Kolts in the shape they were. But as soon as we started some actual upholstering, the license people informed us we were zoned wrong to operate such a business. Mr. Kolt suggested we move the business to his house in South Tucson. I considered Irma Jean a friend and I liked her family, though I saw that there wasn't even enough food in their house to feed Irma Jean's baby.

"Operating out of the Kolts', very soon I came to the realization that Bill Morgen could not upholster, that he frankly knew nothing about it. After talking it over with Mr. Kolt, we decided to hire in an actual upholsterer. The man who answered the ad was named Arizona Mechanic; it was his authentic name, although it made the whole thing sound like a fairy tale."

Smitty's business venture, like his previous spurts of productivity, eventually ended in chaos. He says, "The upholstery shop was in full gear with Arizona Mechanic doing the upholstery. Then, behind my back, Bill asked Arizona Mechanic to go into partnership with him and drop me and Mr. Kolt. He was disgusted anyway with Bill's drinking, so Arizona Mechanic said no and told us about it.

"I decided I'd had enough of the Morgens. I'd given them a house rent-free, food which they never paid for nor were asked to, paid off the balance on their car, hocked all my musical equipment, and in turn, he tried to betray me.

"I then told him it was best to dissolve the partnership, but they could remain in my house until they made other arrangements. I stayed at the Kolts', working day and night, and for a couple of days Bill dropped in occasionally, and the last time he told me he was leaving for Phoenix."

◆

Richie, with his feelings about the south-side crowd, had not been seeing Smitty regularly. He describes Smitty's house on Adams at that time as "a stopping-off place. If someone on the south side wanted to go dick around on Speedway, they'd stop off at Smitty's and get a beer or something. . . . Smitty used them and they used him. He didn't like anybody and was trying to escape from Gretchen. They were creeps, he even told me.

"After a period of time after Gretchen had been hounding him on the phone, keeping track of him every second, every day . . . he told me that she had told him that he had fun all his life and everything he ever wanted he got and she had never had any fun. And now it was her turn and she was going to make him miserable. It kept building up from there and one minute he said that he would kill her and the next he'd dream up stories of throwing acid into her face and things like that, work out little plans like that."

Richie had also talked to Paul. Both believed that Gretchen was "ruining Smitty," and both wanted to help. Paul had access to a quart of sulfuric acid, and Richie was willing—but Smitty would change his mind.

"No," Smitty would say, "it's no good."

During this time, Richie too had problems, but of a different nature. Darlene Kirk, the postman's daughter, was not seriously in love with Richie, and gave no indication that she would be. His friend, Art Meyers, a classmate of Darlene's, remembers their relationship as "kind of one-sided. After Smitty dropped Darlene, Richie was meeting her at Sunset Rollerama. He'd always liked her, he said, and after Smitty was through with her he said he'd like to take a chance at it. Richie invited her out and then several dates followed, but Darlene, more or less recovering from the falling-out with Smitty, didn't really seem to care. Richie was 'weird' she said. 'He's too excited about things, and he doesn't make a lot of sense. But he's sort of fun to be with at times.'

"He got to her," Art recalls, "and they started going around together," after Smitty had moved away from the east-side crowd. "They looked pretty good. It came to the point where he bought her pretty good rings and wrote all kinds of love poetry to her. Then Darlene told me she asked Richie if she ever broke up with him what would he do. He said, 'Baby, I'll make you sorry.'

"Darlene didn't like being threatened, if you know what I mean, like she was being forced to go with him, so she broke it up. She sent the rings back by some other guy. . . ."

Richie asked Smitty for advice. He dictated a message which Smitty wrote down on a strip of cardboard with a grease pencil. The message was supposed to be from someone asking for a meeting with Richie "behind the Enco station to tell you what a whore Darlene is."

In full accord with one another, Smitty then punched Richie several times about the face. Richie says, "My nose was bleeding, my lip was bleeding and my eye was getting black and blue when Smitty dropped me off at Malvern, the corner where Darlene's house was." Richie told Smitty, "I'll need about five minutes before you come in."

Then Richie forced his way into Darlene's house in order to "spill blood on her carpet and her bedspread and the furniture there, and I held up the piece of cardboard and said 'I got the bastard for this.'"

When Smitty arrived he said he'd heard that "Richie damn near killed a guy behind the Enco station," and as he helped Richie out of the Kirk house, he told Darlene, "Richie must really love you, Darlene."

"Just get him out of here!" was Darlene's reply.

◆

For Smitty there came a break in the pressure. Gretchen went to California with her parents on vacation. After the collapse of the upholstery business, Smitty says, "I felt drained and disgusted with people. Gretchen was gone, so I decided to invite all my friends over for parties. For a couple of days Bobby Garcia stayed at my house and he invited his friends as well. I'm not sure how long the parties went on, but the idea lasted for a couple of weeks.

"I'd managed to forget about the Morgens and suddenly Gretchen returns, learns of the parties and is furious with me. As soon as she storms out, Mary French arrives (she had been in Texas) and demands that I marry her because, she claims, she's expecting my baby. Mary called my mother and demanded a large sum of money to take off and have the baby quietly, but my mom doesn't have the money."

The day after Mary left, disgruntled, Richie asked to borrow Smitty's car. He said he was following Darlene Kirk. While Richie was in the house, Smitty received a phone call from Gretchen. When it was finished, Richie says, "He just put the phone down gently and walked into the bathroom. We were all there talking and all of a sudden the door of the bathroom was flying against the heater. It was like the house was going to fall apart and he ran out the back door."

Richie stayed where he was. He says, "Somebody went out back after him and came back in and then I went out and he was out there walking, pacing up and down by his car. I said, 'What's up?' He said she just told him on the phone that when she was over in California she had some relations with a guy over there, and then he went over and sat down on the car and started crying and saying, 'I really loved that,' then I just walked back in. The phone rang again and I picked it up and it was Gretchen and then Smitty yelled through the screen door to give him the phone outside and he sat down outside."

For the next few days, Smitty says, "Everything was fine . . . until Gretchen then decided that *she* was pregnant and wanted to know what I intended to do about it. I said, 'At the moment, nothing.' We got into an argument at her house and she was screaming senselessly so I left. A week passed and on Monday afternoon of August 16th she came to my place and asked me to run away with her, she said we'd elope. I told her no, that I couldn't do that, so she got into her car and slammed the door. She turned around once and yelled, 'Smitty, you rat!' and drove away."

◆

That night of Monday, August 16, *Tickle Me*, starring Elvis Presley and Julie Adams, was playing at the Cactus Drive-In Theatre at 22nd Street and Alvernon. At approximately 7:30, Gretchen, driving a Pontiac Le Mans, left for the movie with Wendy, her thirteen-year-old sister.

Gretchen's mother, Nancy Fritz, had noticed Gretchen's increased restlessness since their return from San Diego, and was especially aware of it that evening while she dressed to attend the theater with her husband, Dr. Fritz. But Gretchen and Wendy left the house before Mrs. Fritz had a chance to talk to her.

During an intermission at the Cactus Drive-In, while

Wendy went to buy refreshments, Shirley Bates came to Gretchen's car. Shirley says, "We talked about Smitty, and I told her someone said he was giving a party . . . but I didn't know who was there. Gretchen got mad about it and didn't say anything else."

The following morning Nancy Fritz discovered that neither Gretchen nor Wendy had returned home. There would have been no real cause for alarm if Gretchen had been alone, but because Wendy had been with her, Mrs. Fritz was worried. She telephoned Gretchen's friends, who said they hadn't seen her, then Mrs. Fritz called Katharine Schmid at Hillcrest.

"I have no idea where she could be," Mrs. Schmid replied. Smitty said he didn't know anything either, but volunteered to check around and ask some of the others.

"You mean she didn't come home at all?" Smitty asked. He placed several phone calls. One was to a sixteen-year-old girl named Gloria Andrews, and he told her that both Fritz girls were missing. Gloria recalls, "He said now he could go out with anyone he wanted to."

Finally Mrs. Fritz called the police. They made a routine check of the neighborhood, then the Cactus Drive-In where Gretchen had said she was going. Nothing turned up and an All-Points Bulletin was issued on the car. The police also visited the houses of friends of both girls, but received no concrete information.

Because of Dr. Fritz's community standing, the police thought that perhaps the girls had been kidnaped. But after several days had passed and no one asked for ransom they dismissed the idea. "They wouldn't wait this long," a detective said. "There'd be no point to it. More than likely they've run away."

Smitty was questioned by the police. He had no information to offer, but suggested that Gretchen had made new friends while she was in San Diego and could have returned there to visit them.

Since the police were familiar with Gretchen as a headstrong, willful girl, they soon thought she had just driven off somewhere, and proceeded with a routine missing-persons investigation, not bothering to check out Smitty's San Diego lead. When they failed to get results, Nancy Fritz hired a private detective, William Helig, who ran a security patrol in Tucson. Supplied with photographs, descriptions, and names of the girls' friends, Helig launched an inquiry. That night, shortly before midnight, four days after the sisters had disappeared, Gretchen's red-and-white Pontiac was found in an annex parking lot of the Flamingo Hotel on Stone Avenue near Speedway.

The speedometer had sixty additional miles on it, but someone had disconnected it. There were traces of gravel and mud on the floor of the front and back seats. The driver's seat had been pushed all the way back. Gretchen's purse, containing $20 and change, two ticket stubs from the Cactus Drive-In, Gretchen's keys, a business card from Smitty's Upholstery venture with Bill Morgen, were also found. This alarmed Nancy Fritz who said, "She would never leave these things."

Helig and city detectives examined the car and made an investigation of the neighborhood around the Flamingo Motel. No one had seen the car being parked.

The next day Range Deputy John Gammons, patrolling the area south of Tucson, received a report that two girls fitting the descriptions of Gretchen and Wendy Fritz had been seen hitchhiking along the Nogales highway. It was reported that the girls were picked up by a car heading toward the Mexican border, some sixty miles south.

With news of the deputy's report, Nancy Fritz was hopeful and asked that Sheriff Raymond Burr send Gammons across the border to find the girls. Burr said he did not have the authority to send a deputy into Mexico, that such an expedition would incur unjustified expense. Dr. Fritz then volunteered expenses and Gammons went to Mexico.

In Nogales, the deputy questioned some of the local inhabitants, showing them pictures of the girls, and more than ten people swore they'd seen them boarding a southbound bus for Hermosillo and Guaymas. Gammons went further into Mexico and westward along the Gulf of California. He met numerous persons who had seen two girls similar to those in question, and the deputy obtained "almost positive identification" in two other tourist towns. He consulted with the Mexican immigration authorities but they had no record of the missing girls' having obtained tourist permits.

Then a Mexican policeman reported he had issued a

traffic citation to two girls answering the descriptions who were driving a Volkswagen the wrong way on a one-way street. The policeman said there was a *turista* sticker on the windshield. This too was checked out by Gammons but with no results.

Some 460 miles further into Mexico, in a resort at Mazatlán, two girls similar to the Fritz sisters had been cited for wearing bikinis around the beach club. Girls of their approximate description had been seen "around some of the teen-age places in the tourist section." Then a report came that they had checked into a motel in another town. Gammons pursued these leads, but found nothing. He was then ordered to return to Tucson by his sheriff, who felt that the deputy could not be spared any longer.

The sheriff's department printed hundreds of handbills in Spanish, with pictures and descriptions of the girls, for distribution south, and arrangements were made with a Mexican newspaper to carry similar notices in hopes of turning up further leads.

Back in Tucson, private detective Helig kept talking to Smitty, who was annoyed by the repeated questioning.

"I even talked to some of the others," Smitty told the detective, "but they haven't any ideas about it. I just don't know what I can tell you further."

"But surely," Helig persisted, "two girls like that wouldn't vanish without someone knowing something about it. You were going steady with her for several months. . . . And she gave you no idea, not even an inclination that she wanted to leave, or was planning to go somewhere?"

"Oh, sure, she was always ready to leave," Smitty said. "She talked about it often, but there was nothing definite, no plans. I said she might have gone back to San Diego, that's really the best I can do."

The day after Gretchen disappeared, Smitty had called Richie. He asked him if the police had been to see him, then told him, according to Richie, that "Gretchen had run away last night and she took Wendy with her and left in the car."

Richie recalls that "Sergeant Wilhelm had been over and left his card. I called Wilhelm, and the only thing I told him was that Gretchen's car drove by my house about 12 o'clock that night, the night they were supposed to have disappeared."

About a week later Richie was sitting in Smitty's living room, drinking beer. Richie says, "He told me that he supposed that I knew what had happened to Gretchen, and I said 'No, I don't,' and then he told me that he had killed Gretchen, and Wendy, and that he had done it right there in the living room of the house where we were at, and that he just didn't care anymore. . . .

"After he killed Gretchen, Wendy was still going 'Ah, ah, ah,' gasping, and then he said it just stopped. He said that he took the bodies and carried them out and put them in the trunk of Gretchen's car and put them in the most obvious place where he could get caught, he just didn't care.

"I wasn't totally convinced that he'd killed Alleen Rowe, but I was fairly certain of it because of that conversation between him and John. The fact that Alleen had disappeared, and I knew she couldn't possibly run away and make it, at her age. After Smitty told me, 'I guess you know what happened to Gretchen,' then I was convinced of Alleen Rowe . . ."

Richie says, "Smitty told me 'that's three, counting Alleen. Each time it gets easier.' "

A few days after this conversation, Richie reports, "Paul came to my house and asked, 'Is there anything Smitty told you that he did to Gretchen?' Smitty had just gone crazy, things like that. The phone rang and I answered it. It was Smitty, and Paul was still on the porch. Smitty told me the reason he kicked Paul out was because Paul was talking about me, and Smitty told him that he, Paul, wasn't going to run Smitty's life, and he'd pick his own friends. I didn't say anything to Paul about Smitty calling."

The official investigation proceeded without results. Nancy Fritz consulted an astrologer who told her the girls were dead. Helig, the private detective, thought Charles Schmid knew more than he was telling. And then a group known as the "Tucson Mafia" entered the case. Arrangements had been made for these underworld figures to put pressure on Schmid in the hope of bringing forth specific information. Schmid had told Helig he believed the girls had gone back to San Diego. If this were true, the Mafia was prepared to deliver Schmid to San Diego to search for the girls.

Smitty received a telephone call and was told that two men would pick him up and bring him to a meeting. They advised him to be ready when they called. Earlier, Smitty had called Richie and others, telling them there was to be a party. But shortly after seven o'clock, before the party was to begin, an automobile with New Jersey plates stopped in front of Smitty's house. One neatly dressed young man came to the door and escorted Smitty to the car. "Since I didn't seem to have much choice anyway," Smitty says, "I went with them."

Some time later, Richie arrived at Smitty's. "The damn house was deserted, so I sat on the curb and after a while Gerry Wells and Frank came by and said, 'Smitty said there's supposed to be a party.' I said, 'He called me up too.' Frank said, 'Well, let's go in.'"

Smitty was driven south of Speedway to an apartment on Alvernon. "They took me upstairs," Smitty says, "and introduced me to some jolly old fat man named Charles "Batts" Battaglia. The Bonnano brothers were there and some others who didn't do anything but sit and sneer at everything that went on.

"At first I thought I was dreaming and had wandered into a movie set at Metro-Goldwyn-Mayer, but no, I was actually in the middle of what everybody referred to as the Mafia and the underworld. Even though I expected to be beaten with a rubber hose or something like that, nothing like that even remotely occurred." Smitty recalls that the eldest Bonnano did most of the talking.

"So you're the famous Smitty," the man said.

"Yes, sir."

"Understand you used to be the big champion in high-school sports."

"Gymnastics," Smitty said.

"What happened to you?"

"Sir?"

"You look like a punk," the man replied, in a friendly way. "Whatta you say for yourself?"

"About what in particular?" Smitty replied.

They wanted to locate Gretchen and her sister, and Smitty recalls, "They wanted me to find them. When I said they were probably in San Diego and to ask a certain boy there, and he would know, if anyone would, the Mafia decided *I* should go there and see if I could find them.

"Next thing they said was that they wanted to talk to Richie Bruns." Then the two men drove Smitty back to East Adams.

By then a few others Smitty had invited to the party had arrived, Jimmy Scott, some girls. Richie says, "They were all sitting around. . . . Smitty comes with two men, both smoking cigars. Smitty started mingling and just shooting the shit, then he came over and said, 'I want to talk to you outside a minute.' We walked outside and the other two guys came out. They got in the car. Smitty and I were talking on the step, and he told me the guys from the Mafia wanted to talk to us, that they wouldn't hurt us. I said, 'What do they want to talk to us about?'"

Smitty relates: "When I told Richie they wanted to

talk to him about Gretchen, he turned white as a sheet and asked me if they had found them and why did they want to talk to him? I told him they seemed decent enough. . . . He asked me again if I was sure they hadn't found them, I just laughed and said, 'If they found them why would they want me to go to California?' "

According to Richie, Smitty told him, "Somebody's hired them to find out where she is. They want me to go to San Diego to look for them—I suggested they might be there." Then, Richie says, "Smitty looked worried. He said, 'What the hell am I going to do in San Diego? What the hell am I supposed to do there?' "

Bruns got in the car with Smitty and when they arrived at the apartment on Alvernon, Richie was no longer impressed. "This Bonnano sitting there talking like he's so smart, saying, 'Gee, we didn't have a hard time finding you.' Why should they have a hard time? All they had to do was look in the phone book, that ain't no detective work."

There were others there but Richie didn't know their names, only that he had seen their pictures in the newspapers in connection with the Mafia. "This one man that did most of the talking," Richie recalls, "said they had been asked by a friend to locate the Fritz girls and that of all the names that came up of people that should know what happened, they had picked me and Smitty." The conversation, Richie says, concerned Smitty going to California to find the girls. "Some old man was sitting there about eighty in his arthritis. They didn't impress me and I wasn't scared of them. They asked me if I knew where Gretchen was and I said 'I couldn't care less.' Then the two people that picked us up at Smitty's house drove us to Johnnie's on Craycroft and Speedway. Left us off there on the Craycroft side and we were walking over to where we used to sit. . . . I asked Smitty what he was going to do when he got to California. Smitty said, 'I guess I'll just have to fake it out as best I can.' Then he said, 'If they turn up we're in pretty bad trouble. I think we ought to talk to Paul.'

"Smitty was shook by the Mafia, believe me. He was worried about the fact that people were looking for the girls.

"We bummed a ride, stopped off at Pine Crest Liquors, got some booze, hitched another ride over to Paul's. We woke him up and were sitting around talking out front. We told him what had happened with the Mafia, and he didn't believe us. Paul thought we were both having delusions, and did not even believe that the Mafia had even contacted us. He said we ought to go home and sleep it off. Then Paul said, 'But if they did, then you better call the FBI, if you're so worried about it.' "

Paul drove them back to Smitty's house, where Smitty called the FBI. Smitty says, "I was unable to reach anyone in the local office. Then . . . I called all the way to Washington, D.C., to get J. Edgar Hoover on the phone but there were complications and he couldn't get through.

"I left Richie back at my house, went next door to my parents' house and told them what had happened, then called the FBI from their house. Again I couldn't reach them, but Richie had called again too and left a message with somebody at their office."

Richie said, "Washington called back and woke the jokers up here in Tucson." About forty-five minutes later Smitty came back to his house. Richie had been thinking.

"We went out," Richie says. "I told him that my neck was in this because the Mafia guys that picked us up said we were lucky that these big-wheel guys didn't just talk. When the other guys come in *they* will do more than talk. And I said to Smitty, 'My neck is in this too now. *I* am supposed to be the one that hates her so much and everybody knows this and if the bodies are found it will be my neck as much as yours, if not more. . . . I suggest we go up there and bury them, if they're laying out there.'"

But, Richie admitted later, "I wasn't really *that* concerned that my neck was in it too, along with Smitty. I wanted to see the bodies. If there's a body laying out in the desert, later on they'd rush out there like vultures. I wasn't so much a vulture, I wanted to find out. It was either a put-up or shut-up deal. If he killed the girls and they're laying out there dead and he knows where they are, he can take me to them. If not, it's just a bunch of crap.

"I said, 'If you see those bodies out there, we better bury them.' He agreed. So I said, 'Let's go.' He said, 'Fine.' That kind of shocked me right there."

Smitty went to his parents' house and got the keys to

their station wagon. They went around behind the nursing home to the tool shed. Richie says, "We went into the shed looking for a shovel but couldn't find one and so we came back over and went to his father's station wagon and there was a shovel, a flat shovel, in the back of the station wagon. It didn't have a point on it, it was the type of shovel you shovel coal with, stuff like that."

Using the station wagon, they drove to Johnnie's on Stone Avenue and stopped for hamburgers to go. Ten minutes or so later Bruns was driving north on River Road, then east to Pontatoc, eating the hamburgers.

Richie recalls, "I completely doubted it when he told me to drive to the old drinking spot. The place was nothing but a spot for making out and drinking booze. He told me to stop the car, we got out, took the shovel out, and he started walking west from where the drinking spot is and walked down a ways and he said he couldn't find her, and then he said, 'Wait a minute, I smell her,' and I walked one way and he walked the other. When I smelled the smell, I knew. . . . In a way I was a little bit afraid, but it was a creepy feeling more than afraid. A creepy feeling, not fear."

They walked down along the wash, and, Richie says, "A couple of seconds later he said, 'Come here,' and I walked over to where he was and he was kneeling down . . . and he just nodded and said, 'That's Gretchen.' And I looked down and there was just a sort of black form down there, and all the ground around it was turned black.

"You couldn't see it when looking over it, because of the black. Looking down on it, at first when I was standing over it, I felt part of the same feeling that someone would feel if they read an obituary of somebody they disliked intensely dying, a type of satisfaction, really. Not pity, not anything of that nature."

Richie examined the body. "I could feel the top, and I felt the hair. It was all like wiry, and that smell was on me all the time. But I couldn't really see it, distinguish it. Looking down over it, being right on top of it, you could strain but you couldn't tell anything. You couldn't distinguish eyes, nose, mouth, teeth; it was just black, looked like something down there.

"And the hair. You could see the bra. The whole blouse was open, and you could see this white of the bra, and see this rag tied around the legs. An old rag, knotted in the center, both legs tied.

"He said, 'Wendy should be up further on the hill,' so he started walking up the hill and a minute later he said, 'Come here,' and I walked up and he said, 'That's Wendy.' It was just a pile of black dirt, looked thrown over something like, it looked like it was bulging up, couldn't make out anything, it was black like somebody had spilled oil there. . . . I could see part of a leg sticking up out of the ground.

"I said, 'We better bury the bodies,' so we walked down past Gretchen to the wash further down the hill where the ground looked the softest . . . tried to dig a grave with the shovel but I couldn't dig with it because the ground was too hard and it didn't have a point. He told me to shovel for a while and he went looking for a softer place.

"I was still trying to shovel. . . . He then came back over and he said we had better move Gretchen because she was lying out in the open on the side of the hill there. He walked back up to where Gretchen was and he grabbed hold of her by a rag tied around the calf of her legs, both legs, and he grabbed ahold of her by that and dragged her down the hill. . . .

"I could see the form, one arm was sticking up, the hand out. It was stiff. It just dragged like that, like a hollow shell, it didn't even look like there was any weight to it. That was grotesque, seeing that. That was like seeing a horror movie.

"He drug her down into the wash part there, under this mesquite tree, dropped it there. We just left Wendy where she was. We started walking back up and he told me that I better go down and wipe her shoes off and wipe some prints off, and he stood there and I walked down and I took out my handkerchief and wiped it over —real quick. Then I walked back up to where he was and he told me to take the shoe off and throw it. At the side of the mound, which was apparently a leg sticking out with a shoe on . . . I took the shoe off and threw it."

Walking back to the car, Richie recalls, "Smitty told me, 'You are in it as deep as I am now.' I don't know what we talked about back at the car, except the car. We were going to say we had decided to go to Phoenix because we were scared (of the Mafia), but had decided to come back."

Richie stayed over at Smitty's house that night. The next day Smitty left early to get a haircut and Richie got up and went through Smitty's record collection. He says, "I took a few records I wanted to borrow, called the old man, and went home."

When Smitty returned from the barber shop he found that the FBI had contacted his parents, had come to the house and left just before he arrived. Smitty says, "The following evening the Mafia called and asked if my suitcase was packed. They said they were coming to pick me up for the trip to California. They seemed nice and polite about everything and on the trip they even gave me $20 for cigarette money. The plan was to check into a motel in San Diego, I'd call the boy that Gretchen knew, we'd find the girls and then return home. They assured me that nothing would happen to Gretchen as far as the law was concerned and everything would be all right.

"As soon as we checked into the motel, I tried to telephone the boy, to get a hold of him, but I was told he wouldn't be home that night. We remained there at the motel and decided that I should show pictures of her around the beach places and try to find anyone that had seen her. I spent the afternoon doing this (spent the $20), walking around the beach places showing the pictures and asking if anyone had seen them or knew their whereabouts, while the two Mafia guys remained at the motel.

"Along about three or four o'clock in the afternoon a bunch of policemen pulled up and said that I was under arrest for impersonating an FBI agent, and while they were taking me to the police station they informed me that I was to be charged with murdering Gretchen and Wendy Fritz.

"I really couldn't believe it, but the cops scared me and at the station I managed to call Tucson and asked my mother for help. The police did not book me though, and I was kept in a holding cell for over an hour until a man came in and asked me if I wanted to take a lie-detector test.

"I said yes, and he took me from the holding cell and into another room. There he left me. Soon another man came in and asked me a few questions and then unexpectedly he released me to go home.

"By then I was really confused. I wanted to take off immediately but I didn't have enough money left, at least not enough for fare back to Tucson, and I didn't know what I was supposed to do about the Mafia men. So I headed back to the motel in hopes of getting some money from them. There didn't seem to be any reason why they'd detain me any longer.

"But they were not at the motel and the manager came to me and said the police had been there moments before, and that they'd removed them from the motel in handcuffs. I quickly went to the nearest phone booth and called my mother collect. I asked her what I should do. She said she'd wire me some money in care of the ticket office at the Greyhound Bus depot, and said I should call her back at 7 o'clock if anything went wrong, and if she didn't hear from me that would mean that I was on my way home. If I did call her back it would mean that I'd been arrested again.

"I really felt mixed up and waited around the bus depot. As soon as the wire finally came I bought a ticket to Tucson and waited some more for the bus. I had a hamburger and some coffee in the diner, then headed for home."

When Smitty was taken to San Diego, his parents went to Richie's house to see whether Richie had also been taken on the ride. They told Richie what had happened and, Richie recalls, "I was surprised he'd gone, since I never thought anything would come of it."

Back in Tucson, Smitty told Richie the Mafia had chased him along the beach, shooting guns after him, and that he had been arrested and held on murder charges. "Smitty said he couldn't find the guy that laid Gretchen over there. He said he was walking around beaches, showing her picture like an ass, playing the role."

For some time, Richie had been going through his "own personal hell," watching Malvern Street and Darlene Kirk's house in an attempt to stop her from going out with other boys. Richie says, "We broke up because of her parents finding out about a so-called *suicide* attempt of mine, but we went together in secret until the stress became too great."

They were saying that Richie broke into Rincon High and jimmied Darlene's locker to get at any notes she'd received from other boys.

Art Meyers recalls that "One night there was holes cut through her screen door and it looked like burglars to Darlene, but her old man was pretty sure it was Richie.

"What happened was that from that day on Richie watched the street twenty-four hours. He had an old '50 Cadillac, and up and down, up and down her street. Without stopping. He climbed trees to watch her, he'd hide behind garbage cans, he even hid inside one and he'd use binoculars. He terrorized the whole neighborhood, everyone was scared of him. Little kids saw the car coming and would run to their yards.

"He's pretty smart about laws and stuff like that, he knows what he's doing and he said he could walk the streets without getting in any trouble. He borrowed Smitty's parents' dog and used that a few times in case anyone showed up to take Darlene out or anywhere. He was carrying a baseball bat and told the police he was just protecting the neighborhood from burglars or that he'd just come from the park where he was playing ball."

Richie says, "It wasn't so bad when I was on the block, but when I was away from it, like I was really hurting. Many times I was running around that block like a nut. I'd see a car, something would happen, I'd take off and I'd get to the point where I couldn't hardly breathe sometimes. I'd get so excited, everywhere at once. . . ."

Smitty had given an account of his San Diego trip to the Tucson police and the FBI. They listened with interest and questioned him some more about Gretchen.

By now the city was filled with wild rumors and lurid stories of what had happened to the Fritz girls. Private detective William Helig still thought there was more information to be obtained from Smitty. His interest had been rearoused by having listened to a tape recording made by Norma Rowe in which she named John Saunders, Mary French, Schmid, and others as having some connection with her daughter's disappearance. Checking further, Helig got hold of Saunders' police record: disorderly conduct, shoplifting, and simple assault. Also, a court summons to answer charges had been sent to Saunders on April 9, 1965, which Saunders had failed to acknowledge. The police found no trace of Saunders, which meant that he'd been out of Tucson at least since April 9th.

Helig requestioned everybody, trying to crowd them into making some sort of move that would lead to more concrete information. He and the police questioned teen-agers over and over, and one of them commented, "Like they can't find anything on their own and are going to pull anything out of somebody like some crazy tooth-happy dentist." Finally, as had happened after the Alleen Rowe disappearance, parents obtained court injunctions barring further harassment of those "being subjected to interrogation. . . ."

Earlier, around September 1st, Paul Graff had moved back into Smitty's house. He needed $180 to get a divorce from his wife, and Smitty sold an insurance policy to get him the money. Smitty's Falcon was still impounded so Paul came along as chauffeur on Smitty's first date with a girl named Diane Lynch.

She was fifteen and lived with her family in a rundown quonset hut on a dirt street in South Tucson. They had come to Arizona from Iowa seven years before. Her father, Buck, had tried to find work as an unskilled laborer. He left his family in Tucson after hearing that Mexicans worked there for 12¢ an hour, when they were able to get work.

Diane's eldest sister, Thelma, married a gas-station attendant at sixteen, leaving Diane the oldest child remaining at home. She had five sisters and two small brothers. It had been the hope of Diane's mother that her daughters would be married by the age of fifteen. Diane attended Amphitheater High School where she knew Gloria Andrews. Gloria knew Smitty.

"One day in the school cafeteria," Diane recalls, "Gloria came up to me and said she wanted to go someplace that night but she didn't have a date. I was going steady with a boy named Mike Delson, so he got her a date and we all doubled to the Hi-Ho to hear some rock 'n' roll.

"Mike and I were not getting along too well and

Gloria could see it. She said she'd return the favor for me sometime by getting me a date and she asked me if I knew Smitty, that everybody knew Smitty. I didn't and then she said that I *had* to go out with him.

"Later she told me, 'If you don't go out with him he'll blackmail me.' Blackmail you how, I asked, and she said she didn't know but he just would. Gloria showed me a picture of Smitty and I thought he was really cute, so I said I'd go out with him, and Gloria was so insistent about it. . . ."

Diane was a slight girl, weighing only eighty-seven pounds, with delicate features and extremely long eyelashes. When Smitty saw her for the first time she seemed to him to be "just my size."

With Paul as chauffer, they went to a Mexican taco café in South Tucson. Smitty thought the tacos were great and Paul drank a lot of beer. Paul made Diane uncomfortable; all his comments seemed to have an edge to them. Smitty concentrated on Diane. The discussion centered on Gloria. Smitty laughed and said she'd called him up and offered him ten dollars if he'd take Diane out for a few nights. "Get to her, make her think you're in love with her, then drop her like a ton of bricks and hurt her real bad," Gloria had said.

It occurred to Diane that Gloria was interested in Mike, and that the date with Smitty was a scheme to make Mike jealous. But Diane liked being with Smitty; though she'd been with him for less than an hour, she thought she'd already fallen in love with him.

Paul dropped them off at Johnnie's on Stone and

said he'd come back later. Smitty and Diane sat by the window and shared coffee and cigarettes. When Paul didn't return they walked hand in hand to Sambo's, another restaurant a few blocks north. "Are you really playing the game Gloria put you up to?" Diane asked. Smitty said, "Of course not," and grinned.

They were eating pancakes when they were approached in Sambo's by an elderly woman wearing Indian jewelry who had been staring at them from the counter. She came to their table and introduced herself as an astrologer, the representative of Universalism and Fortune.

Smitty said he was "absolutely fascinated" and the woman sat down and told them, "You two must never see one another again. And under no circumstances must you marry one another, or for that matter any relatives of your families marry one another." The woman said she had been watching them carefully and could easily see their fortune "as though it's smoke coming off your bodies." If her injunctions were disobeyed, she said, "hard trouble will come of a serious nature." The woman's forebodings spread gloom as the pancake syrup hardened.

They left Sambo's, walked south to Speedway and past the Flamingo Hotel. Smitty stopped Diane and with a smile asked her if she'd care to become his "permanent wife."

Diane says, "I didn't even think it over when he said that. I just said, 'OK.'"

Smitty recalls, "I was so disgusted with everything

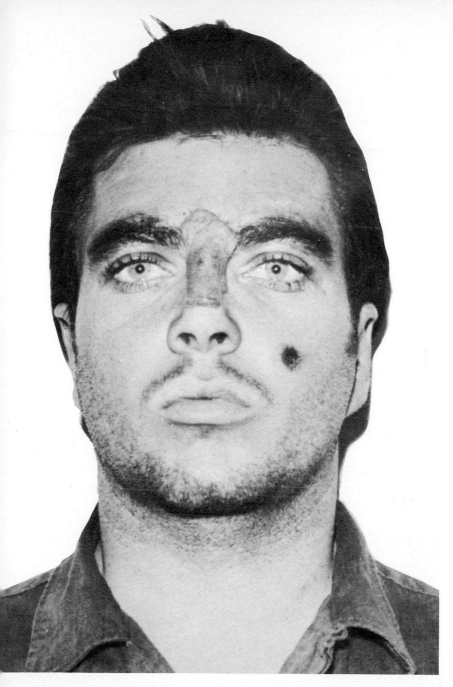

arles Schmid, Jr. — Photograph taken at the time he was booked for the murders
Gretchen and Wendy Fritz.

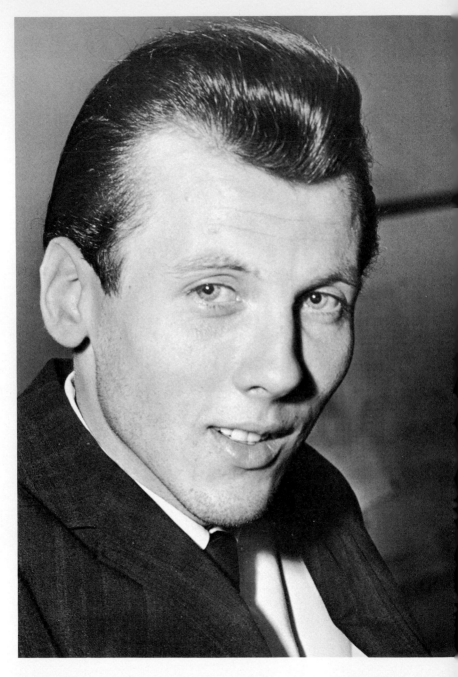

Richie Bruns.

Pebble Productions, I

SPECIAL
Police Bulletin

P. O. BOX 1071
UCSON POLICE DEPARTMENT
TUCSON, ARIZONA

Tucson

Bernard L. Garmire
CHIEF OF POLICE

NORMA ALLEEN ROWE, WAF, DOB 27 October 1948, Dallas, Texas, 120#
blonde hair, brown eyes, fair tanned complexion, white blemish
center of back, small scar right eyebrow, very faint. Missing
since 31 May 1964 at 2230 hours from 7342 Calle Cuernavaca, Tucson,
Arizona. The only clothes at time she left home is a one piece
black bathing suit, blouse with yellow flowers and orange rubber
thongs. Destination unknown.

Any information - Tucson Police Department, Tucson, Arizona,
phone 791-4404 or 791-4411.

Juvenile Detail, Case #276330.

The missing-persons bulletin issued for Alleen Rowe.

Gretchen Fritz (at right) with friends.

Gretchen, the summer before her death.

Nogales, Mexico: Charles Schmid marries Diane Lynch.

Schmid at the Fritz trial.

Schmid's drawing of "Homer the Rat."

A page from Charles Schmid's prison diary.

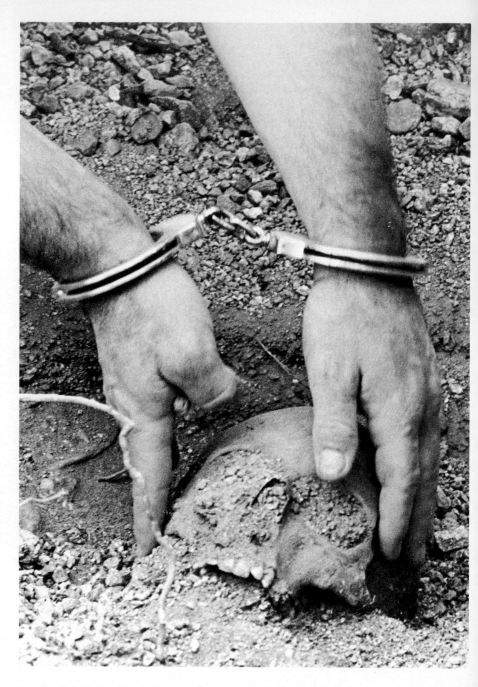

Charles Schmid, manacled, unearthing the skull of Alleen Rowe. *Grasberger*

and everyone I was madder than hell. Life was spinning a hundred miles a second and hurtling all my possessions away from me. I'd sat and figured that in one summer I'd lost what amounted to everything, even the damned cat I had. I can't explain what happened when I met Diane, I only know it did happen and so fast I couldn't really believe it, and it wasn't that I just wanted sex with her. In fact I pushed it back."

They played blackjack and Monopoly at Smitty's house while they were waiting for Paul to come and drive her back to South Tucson. When Paul arrived, according to Smitty, he'd had too much to drink and didn't say a word.

While Paul had been staying at the house, from September 1st until Smitty's first date with Diane, there had been parties. Gloria Andrews, Shirley and Kitty Bates, and others had attended. Paul "made home brew from potatoes and cactus juice," and there was beer from the supermarket. All this ended when Smitty started seeing Diane. He took her to school in the morning and met her in the cafeteria for lunch.

"Before I dropped out," Diane says, "I'd leave during the afternoons with Smitty. He would stay at our house in the evening, watching television, playing with my two smaller brothers. He once ate eleven tacos at one sitting, but usually averaged about seven. I got so I could eat six and we drank Pepsis while we ate.

"Then we'd go to the movies on the weekends at the drive-in where they played five monster pictures, and when the last picture is over the sun is already shining on the screen. They'd let carloads of kids in for one dollar a car.

"Or we'd go over to Smitty's house. Paul had left his home brew stocked in Smitty's refrigerator but nobody liked it—except Richie Bruns. He was there one day walking back and forth in Smitty's house and drinking the home brew Paul had there. Richie asked me questions about my family and walked back out of the house.

"Smitty and Paul had a pretty bad fight after Smitty and I were going out. Paul said, 'How can you marry a whore like that?' and Smitty was so mad he smashed his fist through a wall. Paul's divorce came through and he moved out and went to New Orleans. . . .

"Anybody who needed money, Smitty would give it to them. He gave it to them until he didn't have any left and then they'd get mad. He's a soft touch. If he had ten dollars and you went up to him and said you needed $10, said you had to have it real bad, he'd give it to you. Three-fourths of the $300 a month from Katharine went to his friends, like Richie and Paul."

During this time, Smitty took to wearing a bandage that covered the bridge of his nose. He told his friends, "It happened in a bike accident." Diane rather liked it. Richie says, "That patch on his nose, originally he did a real good job. He looked like he really broke his nose, with that type of splint on it."

With heavy makeup, the fake mole enlarged, "that patch on his nose," and wearing a white dinner jacket and high-collar shirt, Smitty maried Diane on October 24, 1965.

Diane says, "We got married in Nogales. I wore a white satin dress with fur cuffs and a wedding veil. . . . That night, back in Tucson, we had a reception at Katharine's. Jimmy Scott was there, Gerry Wells, and so was Richie Bruns.

"Richie seemed in a daze and just sat there staring at Smitty and me. He said he didn't believe we were married. Katharine and my mother tried to prove it to him, showing him the certificate, but he just refused to accept the facts and wouldn't believe we were married."

Smitty walked outside with Gerry, Jimmy, and Richie, who wanted him to go with them to celebrate the wedding, to leave Diane at home with "the others."

Smitty said to Richie, "I just got married, man. I'd like to spend tonight with my wife."

Richie motioned Smitty to the side, and asked, "How can you do this? You know what's happening?"

"What's happening?" Smitty asked.

Richie said, "I mean . . . the dead girls."

"What 'dead girls,' Richie? What're you talking about?" Smitty said, smiling.

Diane says, "Then Smitty and I drove to Johnnie's. We'd gotten his car out of impoundment and that night we put over 300 miles on it, just driving all around Tucson. Smitty was having fun driving and there just wasn't anything else to do. When we returned to the house we found empty glasses and it was obvious Richie had brought Gerry over and they'd been drinking. But they must not have finished because they took the bottle with them.

"After that we'd invite friends over for dinner, Ronald Baines and Jack Spiers, we used to go on picnics at Sabino with Jimmy Scott and his girl. We'd have spaghetti quite a bit and Smitty wanted French toast for breakfast every morning. Then he'd turn on his stereo and play Elvis Presley records. Morning, noon, and night it was Elvis. Smitty would sing along with the records and then record his own voice singing the Elvis songs.

"Sometimes we would help out at the nursing home, serving food, washing clothes, but not very often, and the rest of the time there wasn't much to do. At nights we would sit home playing cards, Monopoly, or dominoes, or driving around to Johnnie's. He said he'd teach me to play cards real good and we'd take a trip to Las Vegas. . . .

"I loved Smitty very much and we were happy. We'd gotten a charge account at Montgomery Ward's and decided to refurnish the house. Smitty wanted to get the yard in shape. He began by laying a new winter lawn and then setting in bulbs along the walk to the house. . . ."

Part 3

lance of the Kirks on Malvern Street had intensified. It was going on around the clock. He rarely slept. He couldn't eat. At six foot, he weighed 102 pounds. Then he smashed up his old Cadillac. Art Meyers recalls that "One night when he was racing around her house because he thought some guy was showing up to take her out, he smashed his car into an ice-cream truck, and the driver almost died he was so broken up."

The accident occurred at a T-intersection. Richie, circling the block, approached Malvern on Desert Avenue, when the ice-cream truck turned left suddenly off Malvern. Richie smashed the truck broadside.

The driver settled back in the seat, his head raised, and began to moan in an odd way. It looked to Richie "like he was putting on a weird act," and Richie began to laugh. "It was so damn funny," he says, "and I guess I was shocked or something. I began to laugh at the funny way the guy was moaning. Then when the cops were coming, I got out and saw blood all over the guy's seat, and his arms all twisted up."

Richie lost his license for three years because of the accident, but he didn't give up his patrol of Darlene's house. He borrowed Art Meyer's car and continued to circle the block, but when Art heard that he nearly had another accident, he refused to lend him the car again.

Aware of the Lynch family's indigence, Richie suggested that they rent a vacant house across the street from the Kirks'. The rent was too high for them, but Richie said he'd pay half the rent and furnish the place if they would do him a little favor.

Diane says, "He wanted my folks to move in there and he wanted to sit in the front yard for a while every night, and said that if we didn't want him to sit in the yard then he could sit up on the roof for a while." But the Lynch family didn't take the house and Richie was left to his own devices. "People were beginning to talk about it," Diane recalls. "When he was on the sidewalk he'd tell them he was a free citizen on a public street (he'd even tell this to people who were just passing by and didn't care what he was doing). Smitty had given him more money to keep watching Darlene because he couldn't watch her and look for work too."

Darlene's father talked to the police and was told

he'd have to file a complaint. But Mr. Kirk said he would wait a while. "Maybe Bruns will burn himself out." But there was no slackening in Richie's patrols as the weeks progressed. Many times Mr. Kirk wasn't able to see Richie, but he *knew* he was nearby, "hiding behind something."

Richie's vigil had an unnerving effect on his victims. Mr. Kirk says, "One night after about a couple months of it, I got this air pistol (that looked real) and went out there, confronted him on the sidewalk, and said, 'Get the hell away from here or I'll shoot you.' But he said, 'Go ahead, go ahead and shoot, you'd be doing me a favor.' I didn't know what else to do except run back in the house and lock the door."

On another occasion, Mr. Kirk tried to talk Richie out of his mania, "to reason with him." He says, "Only once did I get to talk to him. I guess we talked for about forty-five minutes. I wanted to know just what was going on with him, I wanted to know *why* he was doing it. I listened to him and he said a lot of things, but when it was over I didn't know any more than before we'd talked about it.

"You stand there and listen to him and look into those eyes, and damn, it gives you the strangest feeling." Kirk sighed and shook his head. "I don't know . . . I'm just a common man. How did I get involved in all this?"

Richie never gave up. He says, "Even without a car I was actually keeping track of them. Her brother had a car, and his friends had cars, they could come over and drive her someplace, hide her down on the floorboards, plus all those friends of theirs trying to give me a hard time.

"It really gave me a feeling of satisfaction, having that whole neighborhood terrorized. . . .

"A real thin guy like me, and all those big men over two hundred pounds, with families and all, all scared of me. It was a real feeling of having power, being able to terrorize that whole block of all those people."

But Bruns was beginning to attract too much attention.

Richie says, "When you see cops on every street corner, you could always look around and see a cop, and you know you're being tailed. They started watching my house. Everytime I looked out through the window I could always see a cop, and if I couldn't see one, I'd leave and then I'd see one before I got two or three blocks."

One policeman, Donald Hill, began "to pass the time of day" with Richie, going to and from his vigil at Malvern. During one of these brief conversations, Richie made the mistake of voicing some threats to Hill, concerning the Kirks. Officer Hill jotted them down. They had a case.

On November 3, 1965, Richie appeared in City Court, charged with disorderly conduct after harassment of the Kirk family. The dean from Rincon High, Art Meyers, and other witnesses were called to testify against him. Richie's attorney was John Price, suggested by the

Schmids. According to Richie, Price "looked around and saw all the prosecution witnesses, they were all over the place, and Price figured he'd better make a deal. There was even a uniformed cop waiting there to take me to jail."

Price talked to the judge before the trial and entered a plea of guilty. The lawyer said, "He's been infatuated with the girl to the point of not being able to control himself. . . . All he needs is to get out of town for a while to get over this." The judge agreed.

According to Richie, "The judge talked for about twenty minutes, a big pep talk about when he was a kid, and from there it was arranged that I'd get out of town on the first plane."

Richie was placed on probation for six months, and under the terms of the arrangement he was to leave Tucson for "at least ninety days." The court ordered the records to show that it was the court's understanding that Richie would go to Ohio to live with his grandparents.

Earlier that same day an article appeared in the *Arizona Daily Star,*

. . . TEENAGE GIRLS HAVE DISAPPEARED INTO THIN AIR . . . detectives frankly admit they have no ideas where they have gone. The mothers . . . fear foul play and . . . insisted from the beginning that their daughters were dead.

Regarding Alleen Rowe,

Intensive investigation has failed to give police even a hint as to her whereabouts. While city detectives were doggedly pursuing that case two more girls disappeared.

Gretchen and Wendy Fritz:

"But police still have no leads to the girls. . . ."

The *Daily Star* went on to report that

City detectives have several times questioned a Tucson boy who was known to have been an acquaintance of Alleen Rowe and the oldest Fritz girl, seventeen-year-old Gretchen. Confidential police sources say they believe the underworld was contacted by the parents of one of the missing girls in an effort to find her. They said the mutual acquaintance of the three girls was the person approached and that the youth went to California to find the missing girl but without success. Police have kicked around dozens of theories. . . . Detective Wilhelm admits that it is possible that one or all of the girls could be victims of foul play. But he is generally inclined to believe they are alive.

"There are thousands of reasons why teen-age girls run away," Wilhelm said, "or leave home, and we have absolutely nothing to indicate that these girls' lives were in danger." He pointed to the fact that it would be quite easy for a girl to fix herself up to look older. "She could cut her hair, dye it, use more make-up . . . a girl can make herself look years older," he said. "We have checked out every tip as fast as we get it, but so far we have drawn a blank."

That afternoon Richie was driving around Tucson with Art Meyers. Richie says, "Smitty was coming off a side street there and he saw us driving by. I was sitting shotgun, and saw Smitty. He yelled, 'Richie!' and we pulled over. Smitty pulled up behind. He knew I was going out of town.

Smitty looked dirty and unkempt to Richie. It wasn't the Smitty that Richie had known. "Smitty got out of his car," Richie says. "He looked taller but he was hobbling like a crippled person. He smelled bad. The makeup was caked all over his face and the splint thing that had looked good had got to be just a dirty old bandage, and snot was on his nose."

"Man, you look bad," Richie told him.

Smitty grinned and said, "That's the advantage of being a married man. You don't have to worry about that."

Art drove Richie home in time for supper and Richie packed his clothes for the trip. He says, "Here was a court order saying I couldn't walk down the street anymore, and the first thing Darlene does is get in a car with some friends and comes by my house, and laughs 'Hahahahahaha!' I was very pissed, and I couldn't even eat."

His mother drove Richie to Tucson International airport and he got on a plane for Chicago. He says, "I was kind of sick when I saw Tucson leaving behind me. But I was really pissed off."

The flight from Tucson to O'Hare Field in Chicago took about two hours, and Richie waited there a few hours for a plane to Columbus, Ohio. He drank coffee, and 7-Up, smoked cigarettes, and wandered around the Chicago terminal.

When he got to Columbus, where his grandmother met him at the airport, Richie says, "I felt out of place. What am I doing here? It wasn't right."

Richie didn't think about Darlene "too much" the first night. He spent most of his first day in town looking for a job. "The rest of the time I was just checking the town around there. The second night I started thinking about Darlene. I was feeling kind of pissed."

The second day he wandered around downtown Columbus, "checking the places," but he felt anxious and out of place, "sort of sick the rest of the day." That night, his third in town, facing eighty-seven more similiar nights (according to the court order), he began drinking beer and then went to bed. After lying in bed for what seemed like hours, Richie suddenly "sat straight up and said out loud, 'I can't take it anymore!'"

Richie recalls, "I went bopping out the door and down the steps, and I said to my grandmother, 'I gotta call my old man.'"

His grandmother replied, "It's way late in the morning. What you got to call out there for? What's the matter?"

Richie said, "I can't wait," and then tried to explain to her everything that had happened in Tucson since he became involved with Smitty. It seemed odd to him when he finally put it in words for another person. His grandmother listened but scarcely believed what she was hearing. She said, "Well, wait until morning. You've been drinking."

Richie cried, "He could be out killing someone else!" and called his father in Tucson.

Richie says, "The old man wasn't a bit surprised. He said, 'Now a lot of things make sense. . . . It'll be all right. . . . I'll call.'"

His father said he would "go down" and explain it to the police in Tucson. Within an hour a Tucson detective called back and Richie told him, "Well, there's this guy —a friend of mine, I mean he *was*—and it's about the Fritz sisters, Wendy and Gretchen, and he'd told me he'd killed Alleen Rowe—there was a couple of other people—I mean that helped him do it, you know——"

It sounded awkward and unconvincing over the phone, but he went on, "No, he murdered these girls. . . . Who? His name's Smitty. I mean Schmid. That's right, Charles Schmid."

The detective said, "Would you be willing to come back here to Tucson and show us the bodies?"

"Yes, I would," Richie replied.

Richie then went to bed and slept for a few hours. He said he hadn't slept that well for a long time. The next morning Detective Wilhelm of Tucson and a detective from the Columbus Police Department arrived at the house. His grandmother woke Richie, saying, "The men are here. They're downstairs."

Richie says, "After about fifteen minutes, after I packed, we left and went in a cop car to the police station in downtown Columbus, and I made some short statements promising to go back to Tucson, that it was of my own volition, and show the Tucson police where the bodies were. I filled out one paper for Alleen Rowe, and one for Gretchen and Wendy." Richie told the police that he was doing it because he was the only one who could stop Smitty.

Then they went to a café in Columbus for breakfast. Richie asked, "Where am I going to stay when you get me back?"

Wilhelm replied, "Oh, we have a special place for you."

"Which jail is that?" Richie asked.

"No, we've got a room for you," Wilhelm said.

There was a pause, then Richie asked the question he had been leading up to: "Will I be more or less prosecuted for waiting this long, I mean, for not sort of talking about it before this?"

Wilhelm said, "I'll see to it that you won't be prosecuted. The guy I want is Smitty."

That day, November 9, 1965, a major electrical blackout occurred throughout the east, and Richie and Wilhelm were delayed most of the day at the Columbus airport before they could get a plane for Chicago. At Chicago, there was another wait until Wilhelm was able to get a jet nonstop to Tucson.

"The guy was really cranking time," Richie says. "We made the flight in a little over an hour and a half. It was about 1:30 in the morning when we arrived in Tucson. There were all kinds of detectives waiting there for us.

"We drove to El Rancho shopping center and I got a pack of cigarettes. Then they took me to a motel on Alvernon. Detective Hill," who had handled the case against Richie for harassing Darlene Kirk, "was in a room next to me and another one was in the other room, and there was one sat up with me in my room. I couldn't sleep. I lay there and bullshitted."

They came for Richie between six and seven the next morning and drove to Johnnie's on 22nd for breakfast. Richie had bacon and eggs. As they sat there, more and more detectives kept coming in. "The numbers grew. All the bigwigs were there. The head of the detectives and the guy that takes all the crime pictures." Then the whole group left as a body and drove north on Craycroft to River Road. "Five cops, me, the guy that takes pictures, at first, six in the car, the other guy followed. They drove straight up to Pontatoc. . . .

"On the way up there I was convinced there weren't any bodies. I was scared. They parked and we all got out, and at first I couldn't find them. I almost walked on Wendy, where she was, I didn't even see her.

"At night things had looked different. It had looked to me like Wendy was planted underneath a big bush, and I was looking for a big bush with a big mountain of dirt beside it.

"All of a sudden, I was standing on open ground, and here was skeletons, and bones and everything scattered all over the place. And the hole she'd been dug up in was only a couple of inches deep. So actually what happened was that dirt was thrown over her, and this big mound I was looking for was actually just a little hole, nothing at all.

" 'That's Gretchen,' I said, because I didn't see the mountain of dirt, and I thought this must be Gretchen. The detectives were walking around the desert and I started walking away, because if that had been Gretchen, Wendy would have been up the other way."

A detective knelt and examined the skull. He said, "This looks to me like it would be more like Wendy, don't you think?" He looked up at Richie, who walked back and looked down at the bones. The skull was small. Richie knelt down and happened to raise his eyes past the detective's shoulder. He sensed something familiar—he was facing the wash.

"I looked down and there was the wash down there," Richie says. He got up and started walking. Wilhelm was walking along the other side of the slope, and when he saw where Richie was headed, he started diagonally across the slope, both approaching a mesquite tree from different angles.

Richie called out, "Over here."

"Yes, I see the hair," Wilhelm replied.

Richie says, "They all sort of walked over and stood around and looked for a while. Then they got in a little conference," and Richie was not allowed to hear what they said.

As Detective Hill approached the group, Richie asked, "Would you pick up Darlene now?" Richie then claimed that he had been watching Darlene because he was afraid Smitty would kill her. He said he had informed on Smitty because he couldn't protect her when he was exiled from Tucson.

Hill said, "Talk to them, I'm sure they'll pick her up."

Richie recalls, "They said they'd pick her up if I'd confront Smitty. I said I didn't think it would do any good. I knew Smitty and he wouldn't confess."

The police then drove Richie to the Southeast desert area off Golf Links Road, to see if he could find Alleen Rowe's grave. Smitty had told him where it was, but Richie had never visited the grave. He was unable to find it, and a detective said, "We'll get Saunders and French back here."

♦

The hair surrounding the "old drinking spot" was gathered and put in plastic containers. Fragments of blouses were found, undergarments and a pair of blue-and-black shorts along with a white shoe.

Bones from the first skeleton were collected into plastic sacks by an ambulance attendant, and the second skeleton was placed in a single large plastic bag, then delivered to the Arizona Mortuary. Dr. Louis

Hirsch, the coroner's pathologist, had studied the remains in the desert. He continued his examination at the mortuary, noting that the hands, feet, and several other bones from the skeletons were missing. His conclusion was that the bones were the remains of two young girls, approximate age and height of the Fritz sisters. But he was not able to determine the cause of death.

Detective Lieutenant George Robles, forty-two, a soft-spoken mild-mannered man, one of the few Tucson policemen to have "dropped a man with a bullet," was assigned to arrest Charles Schmid. To avoid spreading the case "throughout the police force and sheriff's offices," Lieutenant Robles, his partner Clarence Dupnik, and Sergeant Wilhelm were given complete charge of the case. They would make all the arrests and control the suspects. Robles says, "I was asked to study the entire case in what seemed like a matter of minutes." County Attorney Norman Green specifically instructed the detectives to "write up no reports in connection with the arrests of Schmid, Saunders, and Mary French."

Robles says, "I went through the files beginning with the disappearance of Alleen Rowe and repenciled Schmid's name, underlining it on page after page, even before the disappearance of the Fritz sisters. I said, what the hell, why wasn't this guy brought in *long* before this?"

Other detectives told him of the injunctions which had prevented them from questioning Schmid further and Robles said, "To hell with injunctions, this guy should've been picked up and held. He was nailed right *here*," he said, underlining Schmid's name again. Robles says, "It made me sick to see the guy's name again and again and again and to realize he'd never been booked even on *suspicion*—it's like a person's hands are tied and you have to sit back and watch it happen. Injunctions, like hell."

It was Robles's belief that if Schmid had been picked up and held following the disappearance of Alleen Rowe the police might have prevented the murders of the Fritz sisters.

That morning, Wednesday, November 10, the twenty-second day of his marriage, Smitty was working in the yard. It was before breakfast. He had planted some bulbs along the walk and started to rake weeds.

Diane was hanging new drapes in the house, which had previously gained a sofa and a modern easy chair from Montgomery Ward's. The past few days Smitty and his father had laid new linoleum in the kitchen. Smitty was planning to paint the house and do something about the loose shingles on the roof. While he was raking weeds and leaves into a pile, Diane took the washing across to the hospital laundry.

Smitty noticed a car on Second pull past the house and head south toward Speedway. A few minutes later he saw the same car come around the other side of the block, turn into an alley and drive behind his parents' house, then slow momentarily at the rear of Smitty's house. Then it went to Second Avenue, came around the corner, and stopped at the curb with the motor idling. Two men were in the front seat.

Smitty thought the Mafia were after him again. As he worked in the yard he continued to notice the car poking around the neighborhood.

From inside her house, Katharine Schmid saw the car and watched it suspiciously. Raising a pair of binoculars she focused on the windshield of the car: the man in the passenger seat was holding a pair of binoculars to his eyes. Katharine stepped back from the window.

Diane loaded the washer and returned to the house. She was taking the garbage out when she saw Smitty pacing back and forth in the alley, looking both ways.

"What's the matter?" Diane asked him.

"Nothing."

"What are you looking for, Smitty?"

"That car," he said, brushing some dirt from his pants. "Didn't you see that car around here?"

"No."

Smitty went around to the front, saying, "Never mind." Diane followed and asked if he was hungry. "I guess I am," he said, "How about French toast?"

About three hours passed. The car with the two men had kept a steady watch on Smitty's house from various places in the neighborhood. It was shortly after 12 o'clock when the telephone rang and Diane went to answer it. "It's Jimmy," she said. Smitty took the phone in the bedroom and Diane heard him laughing as she entered the living room. Then she jumped, startled, as three men came quickly across the front yard and onto the porch. Diane hurried to the door as one of the men thrust it open and said, "Hi, is Smitty here?"

The three pushed themselves into the house. "Where's Smitty?" one of them asked.

Robles recalls, "When I walked through that front door he was talking on the phone and dragged it into the bedroom. I've arrested most of the murderers in Tucson but seeing this guy—the way he looked, the way his face was with all that stuff, makeup, that smudged black mole or whatever it was—I have to admit I was shocked for a moment. Seeing him face to face sort of set me back. Dupnik said, 'He's a nut.'"

The police grabbed the phone from Smitty and asked who he was talking to. Smitty said, "Jimmy," but when the detectives demanded to know who was speaking on the other end, the phone went dead. They seized Smitty and said, "You're under arrest."

"What am I under arrest for?"

"Murder," Dupnik said, "Come on, let's go."

Smitty swung his arm free. "Hey, wait a minute, what the hell is this?"

"No, let's go," Dupnik insisted.

"Who the hell am I supposed to have murdered?"

"You tell us," Robles said as the other detectives jerked Smitty's arms behind his back and locked his wrists in handcuffs. They were hustling him out through the living room when Smitty asked to see his mother.

"No, you're coming now," Robles answered.

Diane yelled, "Smitty!" as they pushed him through the front door and across the yard.

"Get my mom!" Smitty yelled.

They took Smitty out to the car and Robles started back into the house, but Katharine, Robles says, "threw that big body of hers up in the doorway, her arms raised up like this and started with that search warrant stuff, and brackety-brackety-brack, and I said to myself, 'Oh, no, she means business.'

"Charlie was out there hollering 'Call John Price,' so we left. Schmid kept saying, 'Are you guys for real? Prove to me you're city cops. I could be being kidnapped again. Are you city cops?' I said, 'Forget it, Charlie.' "

When they got Smitty to police headquarters, Robles says, "We were walking him through this room, and it's the polygraph room, but we were only going through there to get to another room, and he starts with this, 'Oh, no, I'm not taking anything like that,' and 'You're not getting me to take a polygraph,' and brackety-brack, so I said, 'Forget it, Charlie, we're not giving you any lie-detector.' "

Schmid kept protesting the polygraph, making a speech on the effects and shortcomings of the polygraph test, even as Robles led him into another room and closed the door. Robles said to him, "Forget it, Charlie."

In the small room with a two-way mirror on one wall, the detectives played tapes which Richie had made implicating Smitty in the murders and also accusing Mary French and John Saunders. Smitty made faces and kept saying, "What it this? Are you guys for real? Who is that? What is this?"

Robles says, "We wanted a confession, although I didn't think he'd give it. I took off the tape and said, 'Which side you want to hear—one or three?' He said, 'How about five?' Real smart.

"Then Dupnik said to him, 'You know what you are? You're a psycho.' You ought to have seen old Charlie, he just froze up and his eyes narrowed, mean, he was burning."

Outside in the corridor, Richie was watching through the two-way mirror. Police Chief Garmire came down the hall and took Richie into another room and asked him if he was feeling tired. Richie said no. Then Dupnik came in, and according to Richie "he asked me if I'd go in and confront Smitty. They felt that if I confronted him that possibly he'd confess. Another detective asked, 'Does this guy have anything on you?' I said, 'No.'"

Richie was led into the room with Smitty, "who was sitting in a chair in one corner of the room," Richie says. "One detective was sitting behind a desk and Robles was standing near the door. . . . Smitty and I were looking at each other."

Robles recalls, "They were both glaring at one another. Charlie said to him, 'I know why you're doing this, I know why you're doing all this.'"

Richie remembers, "Dupnik and another detective came in, and this detective said to Smitty, 'Man, if you don't confess this you're going to go out of your mind. You can't keep something like this on your mind.'"

Smitty glanced again at Richie, and said, "I know why you did it."

"Did what?" Richie asked.

"Fingered me."

Richie said, "You would have to have done something for me to finger you."

Smitty made insinuations about Richie, and Dupnik said, "I thought you said this guy doesn't have anything on you?"

"Man, he's just trying to sit there and tell you that *I* did it," Richie said.

"I'll prove my innocence in the trial," Smitty announced. "I'll get a trial and prove it."

A detective said, "Yeah? You might just have to stand trial three times."

Richie looked at Smitty and said, "You're sick, man. You need help."

A uniformed policeman entered the room quickly and said, "Tinney's coming." Richie was hustled from the room and as he went up the steps attorney William Tinney, "carrying his briefcase and looking straight ahead," according to Richie, was on his way down into police headquarters, followed by John Price.

Smitty was booked on two open murder charges at approximately 1:10 that afternoon. The press had gathered but the police kept the photographers back while the booking took place. Then Smitty was asked to remove his boots. He seemed reluctant to do so, as if intimidated by the request. When he took them off he appeared several inches shorter. The photographers crowded around and started snapping pictures. Smitty sat down on the floor and refused to stand up for them.

The contents of his boots filled more than two shoe boxes. There were folded-up rags cushioning flattened beer cans, which were covered over with a wadding of more rags and pieces of cardboard.

At the same time, Chief Garmire called together a hurried press conference and released details of the investigation.

One hour after the booking, Charles Schmid, Jr., was arraigned before Justice of the Peace Toby LaVetter. His attorney, William Tinney, asked him for the court how long he had lived in Tucson. "Twenty-three years," Smitty replied, and that was all he said.

The arraignment lasted half an hour. Tinney tried to invoke a rule banning all but the principals and court officials from the courtroom, but LaVetter denied the motion, saying he believed the rule applied only to a hearing, not an arraignment.

Tinney said, "I think we owe a duty to try for once to have a trial without all the flame and fury we've had in the last twenty-five." He said he wanted to avoid publicity. "I'm only trying to be fair . . . I'm merely trying to avoid prejudice to the defendant's right."

His motion to set a reasonable bond was also denied and Schmid was ordered held without bail until the hearing scheduled for 10 A.M. on December 13, 1965.

Back at Smitty's house, the police had obtained a warrant and started ransacking the place. They dumped the contents of drawers onto the bedroom floor and pulled clothes from the closet. They asked Diane to identify them and she said, "Mine and Smitty's—why, why?"

The detectives took the cushions off of sofas and chairs, reached behind the water heater, picked through laundry. They took Smitty's tapes and a few other odds and ends out to their car.

Finally, Diane asked what they were looking for. "If it's a gun," she said, "I'll give it to you." She quickly found Smitty's .22 and gave it to one of the detectives. The man looked at it impassively.

"A guitar string," he said.

"A what?" Diane asked.

"A guitar string. You know. You seen one around here?"

Diane shook her head. "Were there any strings missing from his guitar?" the detective asked.

"He doesn't have his guitar," she replied.

The detectives kept on looking. Next door two other detectives asked Katharine Schmid about the same item. "There's no guitar strings in this house," she replied. "He never kept his things here, and he doesn't have his guitar at the moment."

"Tell me," one detective said, "were all the strings on his guitar the last time you saw it?' '

"I don't know if there were strings on it or not," Katharine said. "What's the difference?"

The search turned up no guitar strings, and a disgruntled crew of detectives left the premises.

Meanwhile, Richie had been taken to the Alameda Building Detective Officer where he sat and waited. He smoked cigarettes and chewed his fingernails. Some articles found near the spot where the skeletons had been uncovered were presented to him for identification. He was shown a pair of wrap-around sunglasses, resembling a pair Richie had owned, and Richie said, "The last time I saw them was one night in Smitty's car."

Soon a policeman informed him that "Chief Garmire has just gone on the radio to announce the news." The policeman added, "Darlene's been picked up, just to let you know we kept our side of the bargain." Richie sat for another hour. Then Norman Green and Chief Assistant County Attorney William Schafer came in to talk to him.

Richie says, "Schafer was curious, like why were the bodies black, as I'd described about that night. 'What was the black?' he wanted to know. A cop told him it was a natural reaction, it was the chemicals. Schafer was wondering, perhaps it meant they were poisoned or something, and he was particularly curious that the legs were tied—that showed premeditation. A secretary was brought in and I started giving statements. This continued until late and then a cop drove me home.

"He took me to the door and my old lady asked if

they were supposed to keep me there, and he said, 'No, he's free to come and go as he pleases.' "

It was evening now. At the Arizona Mortuary, Dr. Hirsch compared the teeth in the skeletons to charts by a dentist who had done some work on the Fritz sisters. The fillings and surgery performed on Gretchen and Wendy, the dentist reported, matched the fillings and surgery observed in the skeletons. Dr. Fritz had been summoned to identify the clothing found in the desert. That evening he came to the mortuary and looked at the articles. He said it was similiar to the clothing owned by his daughters but he did not know what the girls had been wearing on the night they disappeared.

Meanwhile, Charles, Sr., and Katharine Schmid left their home on East Adams to meet with Tinney in his offices a few miles east on Broadway. It was about eight in the evening when he told them the outcome of a conference he'd had earlier that afternoon with Chief Garmire and County Attorney Norman Green. Katharine Schmid remembers that Tinney told them: "They are determined to do all in their power to put Charles in the gas chamber. They will settle for nothing short of the death sentence."

"What are we going to do?" Katharine asked.

Tinney said he planned to prepare for a long, hard case and that "it might become necessary for me at some point to bring in additional counsel." He also advised them the case would be expensive and that a substantial sum of money was required for the defense.

◆

Within three days of Schmid's arrest, Sheriff Burr had as many as thirty men searching the east desert area for the grave of Alleen Rowe, and the police had traced the whereabouts of John Saunders and Mary French.

While Detective Dupnik flew to Connecticut with a fugitive warrant for Saunders, Lieutenant Robles left for Texas to arrest Mary French. Robles landed in Temple, Texas, and went by taxi to Belton. He didn't have a warrant with him and made arrangements to have one wired to Belton.

"The police department in Belton," Robles recalls, "was in one room, and the fire department across the hall in another room." He asked to speak to the chief of police, but was told, "Gus isn't here right now. What's the problem?"

Robles didn't want to discuss his business without a warrant, and only asked for the address of the French family. The man at the desk insisted on knowing what business Robles had in Belton. Finally, Robles located Gus, the police chief, and told him that he was there to talk to Mary French concerning a runaway girl from Tucson. The chief said, "You come all the way down here about a runaway?"

The chief said he'd "send Lou up the road to see if

the Frenches lived there." Robles wanted to accompany Lou.

"He'll just see if she's there and come on back and tell us," the chief said. "You don't have to go up there with him."

Robles said, "I'd prefer to. I'll go with him."

The French house looked like part of a project, similar to the place they had occupied in Tucson. Robles thought they'd recently moved in because there wasn't any furniture in the front room. Mary's mother answered the door and appeared unconcerned, even though she asked, "You come all the way from Tucson just to ask about her? Haven't they found that girl yet? Isn't that something. Well, Mary's taking a shower."

Mrs. French went into another room and Robles heard her call, "There's a detective here from Tucson, Mary, wants to talk about that missing Rowe girl or whatever her name is."

Robles waited for a long while. He says, "It seemed like I waited and waited, and all the while I was thinking that Mary might have snuck out the bathroom window." Finally, Mary came out of the bathroom with a towel wrapped around her wet hair. She appeared indifferent.

"I'd like to ask you a couple of things about Alleen Rowe, Mary," Robles said.

"Oh," Mary replied.

"Maybe it would be better if you got something on

and we could go over to the sheriff's and talk a little better over there."

"Oh." Mary shrugged and went back into the bathroom. She closed the door and Robles heard the water running.

Robles waited again. He says, "All the mother had to do was say, 'Like hell you're taking her anywhere,' or 'She's not talking about anything without a lawyer here.' So I had to play it very cool. The last thing I was about to do was even breathe a word of murder or arrest or anything like that."

Mary came out of the bathroom slowly, wearing a dress. "Where are we going?" she asked.

"I thought we could probably talk better out of the house, you know," Robles replied.

Mary shrugged and told her mother she was going out. The mother walked to the door, wiping her hands on a kitchen towel. "They haven't found that girl yet?" she asked.

"I don't even know an Alleen Rowe," Mary said. "I don't know what I can say to you."

"We'll just talk a little," Robles said.

At the sheriff's office, Robles left Mary in one room and told the sheriff the real story. He said he was expecting a warrant to be wired and that the girl was to be charged as an accomplice in a homicide.

Back in the room with Mary, Robles talked to her for a while, "just nonsense," he recalls, "talking about nothing. She kept saying she didn't know Alleen Rowe or anything about her disappearance. She'd answer questions but would volunteer nothing on her own."

Meanwhile, the sheriff sent for the justice of the peace, a small man who was also the town's barber, so that he could prepare for the extradition proceedings. The warrant finally arrived, and the judge asked, out of curiosity, if he could sit in on the questioning. Robles agreed, realizing that the judge would be the best possible witness to a statement. He returned to Mary, who was getting bored, and talked to her for "a few more minutes before laying it on the line."

"OK, Mary," Robles said, "Let's knock off the nonsense. I'm here to talk about Alleen Rowe and you've been implicated in her death—you, Charlie, and John Saunders."

Mary didn't cooperate. Robles recalls, "Out of all the people I've questioned on the Schmid case, out of all those people, Mary is just about the coldest person I've ever talked to. Like ice."

Finally, Robles said to Mary, "You know Smitty got married, you know that?"

Robles says, "It was the only reaction I got out of her, she just changed for a split second. I could see it really got to her. Then she told the whole story, once again answering questions, everything, but volunteering nothing. The statement was five pages, single-spaced. Mary was sitting to my right side, I was sitting and punching the typewriter and the judge was back in the chair near the door.

"Mary's story was pretty close to what Bruns had

said Charlie told him, but Mary got into all the details.

Smitty had wanted to kill someone, a girl, Mary told Robles, just to see what it felt like and to see if he could get away with it. He used Mary to lure Alleen Rowe from the house and into the car with Smitty and John. Smitty drove to the desert where he and John killed Alleen. Mary told the detective that she had not been present when Alleen was killed, but that Smitty told her how they'd done it, with a rock, and then Mary helped them bury the body.

Robles later said, "Naturally, I had to pry the details out of Mary, not that she wasn't willing to talk, but you just have to pry everything out of her."

Mary was put in jail at the sheriff's office and her father came down with Mary's suitcase. "It was a big suitcase," Robles says, "and packed full of everything the girl owned, it seemed."

Mary's father was worried and kept asking, "What's going to happen to her?" Robles told him only that she'd be taken back to Tucson, "to talk some more there."

Mrs. French did not come to see her daughter in jail, but she commented, "If she played the game, she'll have to pay the piper."

Later, at the airport in Temple, Texas, Mary went into the toilet and Robles waited for twenty minutes before rapping on the rest room door. He recalls, "The thought that she'd taken off out a rear window scared hell out of me." But Mary was still there, smoking a cigarette. "We gotta go," Robles called to her.

He had trouble catching a flight out of Dallas, and Mary kept dragging her feet, falling behind. Every few minutes Robles had to say, "Come on, Mary, we gotta go. Come on, Mary, we gotta go."

"Oh," was all Mary ever said.

♦

John Saunders was located at his sister's home in Northford, Connecticut, where he was working as a carpenter's helper. He was arrested there by Dupnik and returned to Tucson on a fugitive warrant. He confessed to being an accomplice in the murder of Alleen Rowe, but maintained that Smitty had done the actual killing.

While a crowd of officials and newsmen were waiting at the Tucson airport for the detective's arrival with Saunders, Dupnik left the plane as it made its stop in Phoenix. There, a single car was waiting for them.

They drove from Phoenix to Tucson and went directly to the desert, where Saunders was led out to the wash to show police the grave of Alleen Rowe. But he could not find it.

Detective Wilhelm met Mary and Robles as they stepped off the American Airlines Astrojet. One newsman asked the girl, "Are you Mary French?" but she turned away and settled with Robles in the rear seat of Wilhelm's car.

Soon they arrived at the desert where Saunders had been unable to find the grave. Detectives carrying shovels trailed Mary as she wandered through the cactus. She walked down the sloping bank of the wash then turned west and started hunting for landmarks. Flashbulbs splashed her pale face at almost every step. The earth in the area had already been turned up where Saunders had indicated several possible sites for the grave. Mary appeared uncertain. She marked one site and, when nothing was found, looked again and came up with another two hundred yards away. After hours of digging and finding only some rusty beer cans and two rusted hair curlers, one officer shrugged off the search and said they had "been led on a wild-goose chase." Another referred hopefully to the hair curlers and said, "We'll ask Norma Rowe if these belonged to her daughter."

A confusion of flashbulbs and reporters with tape recorders greeted Smitty, Saunders, and Mary French when they entered the courtroom building for their arraignment for the murder of Alleen Rowe. None of the defendants said anything in court. Saunders looked frightened, barely moving a muscle, and Mary French cried, turning from reporters to hide behind Detective Robles.

Saunders was represented by a court-appointed attorney, Edward Morgan. Mary had no counsel, but a motion that the proceedings be postponed until she could be represented was denied, along with Tinney's motion that the courtroom be cleared of reporters and spectators.

Morgan said he wouldn't allow his client, Saunders,

to continue looking for the remains of Alleen Rowe. He
and Tinney both asked that separate hearings be set
for the defendants and this motion was also denied.
The same day Superior Court Judge Roylston denied
a petition by Tinney for a temporary restraining order
against the Tucson newspapers to black out further
coverage of the charges against Schmid.

Norma Rowe's suspicions had been confirmed. During
an interview she granted on the day of arraignment,
she said, "After all, I knew what happened eighteen
months ago—that my daughter was murdered by thrill-
seeking teen-agers, but I couldn't convince anybody
else.

"Alleen had been invited, coaxed, and finally ordered
to join the sex club," Mrs. Rowe went on. "And this
wasn't just something Alleen dreamed up. 'The club's
the thing,' she said. 'You've got to belong to be in.' But
Alleen had apparently made up her mind that she
wanted nothing to do with the 'in' group, and I think
she was trying to either get back out or stay out when
she was murdered. And this club is still in operation.
A lot of kids are out of town, but there is still a club.
I think the murderers either took her out to the desert
to get her into the group and she refused or she already
knew too much and they decided to kill her when she
wouldn't go along with them. . . ."

Mrs. Rowe spoke with no visible emotion. She named
a boy in a southern state and a girl living in the Mid-
west as additional suspects in the murder of Alleen. "I
have given both these names to the police and one of

the detectives even told me that he thought the boy was in on Alleen's disappearance. But I don't think they have tried to track them down. Alleen was trying to avoid this bunch of creeps, she had been seeing a fellow from the university—a concert violinist. She died wearing his ring."

Norma Rowe's charges shocked many people into believing that an elaborate conspiracy existed, and daily stories on the case kept public interest at a high pitch.

Newspapers and broadcasts following the arrests of the suspects gave detailed approximations as to how and why the murders were committed. Chief Garmire had released stories that ". . . Schmid met the girls on the night they disappeared and drove with them in the family car, the vehicle they had left home in to attend a drive-in movie. In a quiet part of the city, the source said, the car was stopped and while Gretchen was out of the auto her sister was strangled inside. When Gretchen returned, she too was strangled."

A television broadcast reported, "Police Chief Garmire says the motive for the slaying of the three young girls was jealousy stemming from a conspiracy among a teen-age clique. . . . Detectives are investigating the possibility that the Fritz sisters were killed because they knew about the slaying of Miss Rowe."

Publicity became a major issue in the case. Public interest was fed by the further stories on the search for Alleen Rowe's body. The sheriff's deputies continued to dig. Every possible place near the wash was unearthed and for days dozens of police and newsmen tramped through the desert with shovels and metal detectors, finding nothing.

Then a legion of high-school students aided in the search. They seemed on a party treasure hunt, digging with their hands, children's shovels and broken motorcycle fenders. They kept their strength up with hamburgers, Cokes, and trips to drive-ins for french fries and malts. One girl showed up with soup spoons from Johnnie's Drive-in, explaining: "We're looking for a body that's been buried for a long time, I guess, and it's probably fallen all apart and things."

They found objects and brought them to the sheriff: old shotgun shells, a soleless shoe, some reddish rocks with a bit of animal bone embedded in them. The search spread under overcast skies to several hundred yards of desert; bulldozers and other heavy equipment of the Burris-White Machinery Company were employed and soon the wash was pocked with gouges so that it resembled a field that had been worked over by a battery of mortars.

The sheriff told reporters that he was beginning to think the grave had been moved, and Mrs. Rowe thought so too. Nevertheless, she said, the rusty hair curlers originally found were Alleen's. "I'm sure they were hers," she told the press. "There is no doubt in my mind. She and I used the same long bobby pins. There is one girl in a million who uses those long pins like that."

The police began to develop their case, and kept the press informed of everything they found. Irma

Jean Kolt was reported missing, then telephoned from California to say that she was staying there with Shirley Bates. Irma Jean discussed the diary Smitty had told her about, and Sheriff Burr said that he had received numerous phone calls about a diary belonging to Gretchen. Those callers told us that if we got Gretchen's diary, we would get considerable information on these murder cases."

Mrs. Kolt told reporters, "Irma Jean knew a few more things than she should have. . . . There are too many people involved and this thing is really spreading out. Irma Jean and her friends knew about these parties and that is why I forbade her to run around with Smitty. . . .

"Charlie sat in my living room and said that some day he was going to kill Gretchen because she was holding something over his head . . . and when the Fritz girls disappeared my daughter said to me, 'You want to bet they'll never find Gretchen alive?' "

The news media stressed the importance of the diary, as a motive for the murders. "Where is the missing link?" they asked.

The police came to Smitty's house looking for the diary, turning everything upside down, even taking his television set apart. They didn't find it.

By now the murder was one of Tucson's better-known tourist attractions and there was a steady stream of cars past Smitty's house, the supposed grave site of Alleen Rowe, and among the rubble where the Fritz sisters' skeletons had been found.

Sheriff Burr now held to the theory that tropical storm Tillie had carried away the Rowe girl's remains in September 1964. County Attorney Norman Green made it clear that he would proceed with his case with or without a body, citing a ruling in a similar case that made this possible.

The Schmid case received national attention. Reporters from both coasts were visiting Tucson. A *Time* magazine article under the title "Secrets in the Sand," appeared with all the details. Other national publications were interested, and Tucson began to complain about this blemish on its image as a healthy place, "full of sunshine and dry air."

Then on November 23, 1965, in an action perhaps unprecedented in U.S. courts, Superior Court Judge Richard Roylston approved an injunction requested by William Tinney that prohibited police and sheriff's officers, the county attorney and his deputies, from any further discussion of the Schmid case with the news media. Judge Roylston declined, at the same time, to issue an injunction forbidding the press from discussing the murders at all. "In effect," the Tucson *Citizen* reported, Roylston "put news media on probation."

Roylston said he feared that continued news reports of recent "quantity and quality" would prejudice Schmid's case. He could only guess what higher courts would do when faced squarely with the issue of the "conflict between free press and fair trial," but said that he felt the courts would eventually be compelled to set forth new guideposts as to how much the press could be told in advance of a trial.

Commenting on Tinney's request for a news blackout, Judge Roylston said, "If I grant it, silencing both press and law authorities, I'll be infringing on the rights of the press. If I don't, I'll be infringing on the rights of this defendant to an impartial trial by jury . . . if news coverage is continued as it has been, the defendant's right to a fair trial will be impaired. It is conceivable that the high courts would say that the defendant is unable to get a fair trial in any county of a state due to pretrial publicity, and free the defendant, just because his rights have been violated to such an extent as to make an impartial trial impossible."

The public and press were not admitted to the pretrial hearing.

The small glass window on the courtroom door was covered with black paper and taped from within. A window at the rear of the courtroom, left open for ventilation, was guarded by a deputy who shook his head at the few newsmen below, then closed the blinds.

In the room, the defendants and their witnesses were sworn in and ordered not to discuss the case with anyone. The prosecutor did not present his witnesses at the opening of the hearing.

As Smitty stood before the bench in a baggy double-breasted suit, he was still nursing a hope that the charges against him would be dropped. This collapsed when Norman Green announced on November 24th that Saunders would plead guilty to first-degree murder and Mary French would plead guilty to reduced charges. Attorneys for both defendants told the court that their clients would testify for the state against Schmid.

"It's obvious that somebody made a deal," Tinney said. "This has been going on since November 10th."

Saunders's attorney, Morgan, was asked why he let his client plead guilty to first instead of second-degree murder. He said, "If a person is sentenced to life in Arizona, he could be eligible for parole in about seven years. Second-degree murder carries a sentence ranging from a 10-year minimum to life imprisonment."

The preliminary hearing on the two murder charges against Schmid lasted three and one-half days. On November 30th he was bound over for trial in Superior Court.

At the close of the hearing Justice of the Peace LaVetter commented, "I didn't learn anything new from the hearing that I hadn't already read in the newspapers. I've been asked why I bound Schmid over, but all the state has to do at a preliminary hearing is produce probable cause to believe that a crime was committed." He said the state had done this, but added, "It's certainly not one of the best cases in the world. In fact it's one of the worst."

One week later John Saunders was sentenced in Superior Court by Judge Collins. He received life imprisonment and would be eligible for parole in seven years.

Judge Roylston sentenced Mary French on two

charges, of being an accessory to murder and concealing and compounding a felony, but let her serve them concurrently. She would be eligible for parole in four to five years.

Schmid was scheduled to be tried in Superior Court on February 15, 1966, for the murders of Gretchen and Wendy Fritz.

Norman Green made it clear that the state would settle for nothing short of the death penalty.

Part 4

MY DEAREST DI-
ane, Oh, honey, I miss you so much, I want to hold
you and make love to you and have a Christmas tree
and a snowball fight. I want to go on all the rides at
an amusement park and go back east to see your
friends and grandparents, and start a band, and
especially go see Country & Western stars, and go to
Hawaii and California, and play in the ocean with
you. I want to play cards and miniature golf with
you, and race cars, and laugh and cry, and do what
we want and even have a couple of kids.

Believe it or not I really want some kids some day
after we've done everything we want. It will make
our love even stronger, if that's even possible. Just
think, the kids will be ours, all ours. Damn will they

be dolls. I hope you want kids someday because I really and truly do. A kid will be the greatest gift besides your love you could ever give me. I want to get your dad a farm and see them happy and take your sisters out and have parties once in a while and go walking in the rain with you, some hot summer day and get soaked and not give a damn and laugh and smile and make you happy & just do what we want with no one telling us what to do.

I want to send you flowers every day and eat French toast and listen to records and cut our own songs and records and make my parents and yours happy. I want to take you to Mardi Gras in New Orleans and get lost with you in all the fun and excitement. I want to do everything we had planned for us and even more because that's the way I am. I've got to have fun and have a blast whenever we can because life is short and we deserve to be happy. I want to dance with you and tell you jokes, and do silly stupid things just for fun. I want to run down the street at 12 midnight and wake people up just to tell them I love you.

Just when we got a car and enough money to do these things *this* crap has to happen. Why, we'll never know. . . .

Enclosed by a steel cyclone fence, the windowless one-story Pima County Jail building sits on the desert west of Tucson like a cement box.

From Cell 14, Tank E, Charles Schmid wrote a

letter to his wife almost every day while awaiting trial. He repeatedly insisted on his innocence to Diane, who had no way of knowing the facts. It seemed at times as if he was trying to convince himself, like most confined men cut off from their ways of life.

Smitty continued in his letter,

Maybe it happened so when I get out we'll have even more fun and appreciate everything more. We just started to have fun and the real blast was just beginning. Fate slipped up on me and took it away, but someday I know I'll be found innocent. Even if it's after they kill me at least you'll know I loved you, and what I wanted, and more of what I'm like. For better or worse, darling, this is what I'm like. If nothing else at least I gave you all I had. I just know I'll be out soon and in your arms and we'll be doing a hundred million more things than what I've said we'd do. When I get out I don't want to waste a minute.

All Smitty's past outlets for expressing himself, except for Diane and his parents, had been silenced at the advice of his attorney, William Tinney.

On a Thursday he wrote,

What do you do everyday? I get up, eat, then vomit, go to sleep, then go to mail call, go back to sleep or play cards till lunch, throw up some more, go back to sleep and pray some miracle will happen so I can see you for a little while, then go to garbage, I mean supper, then play cards and hope I'll see you or somebody, then I go to my cell and crawl under my cot. I won't sleep on that damn steel bed because the light hurts my eyes. I usually stay up all night and draw pictures or write you letters. Write and tell me what you do everyday . . . and what you think about kids. It wouldn't be till we're both ready though, after we have our fun. Oh, damn, honey, I'm not an animal to be caged up like I am. I have to be free. I'm going crazy. Please write everyday and say you love me and dream about me. . . . You can't imagine what this lonely hell is like in here. I'm made to love and be with you. Every day I wonder if I'll ever see you again. I've told them I'll take a lie-detector or truth serum but they don't care. I can't say anything more except if I live or die at least you know I love you. Maybe they have guitars in heaven. All my love forever given, *Smitty*.

♦

Blue Monday Dec 13, you can't imagine how I miss you this close to Christmas. . . . They lied terribly in court today, but I still believe they'll believe *me*. You thought you were sneaky coming down to court today but I saw you going into the girls' rest room.

NO more! I mean it. They're not going to find out who you are. . . .

◆

. . . Since you couldn't kiss me good night last night, Homer did! Don't believe me? I've got a big hickey to prove it, right on my neck. Did you get the drawing of Homer? He comes up out of the plumbing at night, the pipes are so clogged with crap he stinks like hell sometimes.

The preliminary hearing is over [for Rowe]. Friday I go to see when I go to trial. Are your Christmas lights turned on yet? Do you think it'll snow? What should we get Homer for a present? I'm hip, a girl friend. Maybe Homer should be called Homerette—he's pregnant. Not by me, honest. What do you give baby rats to eat? Do they eat people? If they do I'll probably be first! I hope you have a happy birthday. . . . Don't worry, everything is going OK, I mean it. Your handsome, skinny, adorable proud god-father of seven baby rats, *Smitty*.

◆

Schmid would stand trial for the murder of Alleen Rowe on March 15, 1966, thirty days following the trial scheduled for the Fritz murders. Again Norman Green made it clear that the state would ask the death penalty.

Smitty wrote in early January, ". . . I feel real weird,"

I really don't know why though. I saw Bill [Tinney] today, he even looked worried. I've got the awfulest feeling something's up. I don't know what tho. I sure hope everything works out. I feel so empty and mixed up, I guess it's just one of those times. Tension is building again. I miss you. Bill says the lie detector and sodium pentathol wouldn't be admissible in court. I guess that's taken care of. Sometimes I wonder if he knows what the hell he's talking about. He sure does lie to me. I really don't like him worth a damn. I'll keep him though. I'll bet money he'll screw everything up in court. Since he's so determined to keep everything from me I've lost all my respect for him. Why should he care anyway—he's already got all the publicity he needs, and he's already paid so naturally he'll lose interest. Maybe I'm wrong. I hope so. Anyway there's not much I can do. I'll just continue to be his little tinker toy.

I sure love and miss you. I'm afraid all this crap has changed me inside. Lately I've lost respect for everything, except you. I feel so damn mad at everything. I'll probably go to sleep tonight and everything will be back to normal tomorrow. . . . All I can think of to say is that I love you and miss you more than ever right now.

Every night when we get together again we're going to lie in bed and smoke cigarettes and tell each other what the happiest moments of our lives were that day.

3 or 4 A.M. . . . Oh honey I can't sleep worth a damn. You're the only one who can understand anything about me. I can't get the thought out of my head that I'll be found innocent. I know I will . . . I want to be happy with you but this hate I've got might ruin it. I'm just sick and tired of accepting all their crap without fighting back. You're the one decent thing I've got left out of this mess. If you love me as much as you say you do, and I know you do, then help me forget them or this hate will ruin our chance for happiness. Maybe if I'm with you and away from all these cruddy people I'll feel different, but right now I feel different than I *ever* have in my life. . . .

◆

Unbelievable Thurs. . . . Oh, honey, you'll never believe what I'm going to tell you, not even in your wildest dreams. You had just left yesterday when I got a message from this lady I know.

She is a singing instructor and her name is Helen, and she lives on Drexel. I think I showed you the house, a purple one. Well, a long time ago I'd taken a couple of singing lessons from her and she taped my voice. She lives in Los Angeles now and she saw my name and pictures in the paper. I got to know her real well and sent her a Xmas card and flowers for her birthday last year. She's fifty-seven years old. She always thought I was polite and a doll and that I had a real tuff voice. When she saw I was in trouble and she thought I might need money for help, so she took my tapes to a friend of hers who works at RCA recording studios in Hollywood. He listened to them and looked at my pictures in the paper and told her if I could get out of this mess he will arrange an audition. He also said the publicity I had gotten would be great, because if I'm found not guilty people will think I've gotten a rotten deal and want to give me a chance. Won't that be great! All my life I've waited for this chance.

He really thinks I've got a tuff voice. Can you believe it! I've got to get out of this mess!

Baby just think, maybe everyone will love me instead of hate me and I'd be so proud telling everyone you're my wife and they can eat shit!

Maybe this is the answer to our prayers, we'll have money, fame, clothes, cars, houses—for your parents and mine, and most of all we'll have each other. I just can't believe it!

I sure miss decking out in my Continentals and vest and high-collar shirts like I used to, Baby. People will think we're the tuffest couple anywhere. . . . Soon we'll be together and on our way to a fairyland life.

I can't especially wait to tell every girl who wants me to get lost because I've got the cutest, sexiest, and best wife in the whole world. ALL MY LOVE forever given to the most wonderful wife in the world, who, without her letters and courage I'd never make it. Your soon to be the next Elvis Presley, except I'll be better . . . *Smitty*.

♦

He advised Diane to start saving $25 a week.

We'll need a little to go to California for the audition. We're still going back east first, tho, for a couple of weeks just to meet your friends & grandparents and have a little fun because we'll be pretty busy after I start cutting the songs. Damn I can't wait to get out!
   You sure looked sharp Thursday. How did you know I dig sexy, sheer black stockings. . . . I really eat up on the way you dress, from your hair to your pointed-toe black high heels and ALL that's bitchin in between. . . . If you see any shoes or high-collar shirts I might dig, pick up on them. . . . Your soon to be famous husband . . .

Smitty continued to proclaim his love for Diane. Since his marriage had been a desperate attempt to create some stability at the center of his life, he meant much of what he was saying. But again this was one isolated part of his life, and he forgot the times he had repeated the same words on more cynical occasions.

In the middle of January he wrote,

I'm so damn glad you don't want kids. I've got to do so, so many things first. Don't expect me to be a model husband and be meek and mousy and quiet all the time. I'm just not that way. But you already know that. Don't expect me to settle down in one place too long. I'm MAD and ANGRY with people but I'll laugh at them. I've *got* to have a really tuff car again! and a cycle. I've got to have my band and sing again. If this RCA audition falls through, I'll try again and again and again until I prove I'm good enough to cut my songs. I know I can. And I think the audition will prove it. . . . I'll make it big or I won't make it at all. We'll either be rich or poor, I won't settle for middle road anymore. It's not worth it. . . .

All my life I was either a big success or a big failure. Everything's got messed up when I compromised and took the middle road to sacrifice everything for my rotten friends. . . . I hope you understand because I need you badly (I haven't got anybody else). . . .

♦

Well, doll, it seems to be getting a little bit worse than before, but don't worry, there's always a rainbow after every storm.

It's about 10 or eleven P.M. and it sounds like

rain out. You know, it's funny but we've never been together in the rain yet. Someday or even night we'll lay in bed and the rain will patter down on the roof and I'll look at you and tell you how much I love you in a thousand different ways, and be so glad I married you. It seems like we've been married for a long time to me right now. The rain sort of makes me sad but most of all it makes me wish I was in your arms and telling you a hundred different things.

♦

I'm here listening to the radio and all they play is shitty opera, and you know how I hate that. I hope you won't forget to call those people (Tucson *American*) but of course you won't.

Do you know I've been locked up almost three months now? I feel like I'm all drained out inside. It's like I'm dead inside. I really want to GO GO GO! when I'm finally freed. It seems funny how all my friends are really helping right now. It's about time. Maybe everyone will find out what a rotten rat ding-dong Richie really is.

I sure did like that tuff outfit you had on. That necklace was just the crowning touch to make you look great. At least I sure as hell won't be ashamed to take you anywhere, especially to the recording audition! Ha ha!

♦

On the night of February 14, Schmid wrote:

Well, tomorrow kangaroo court begins. I wonder
if they'll sell tickets? Just imagine, 'Ladies and Gentlemen, we now present the biggest farce in history.'
Oh, well, maybe they have guitars and bitchin cars
in heaven. All I'd have to do then is wait for you
and everything would be great.

Did you dye your wig yet? I'll bet it looks great.
Did you know everyone thought you looked like
Mary French? I didn't think so. . . .

Come down Wed night if you want. Don't ever
forget that if something goes wrong and some idiot
tries to shoot me on the way to court and kills me,
that I love you and at least I *was* true to you, even
though I wasn't to anyone else and you made me
happier than I've ever been in my life.

◆

Smitty looked like a new man when he entered the
Pima County Courthouse on Tuesday morning, February 15, 1966. He wore a white shirt, a conservative
black-and-brown tie, charcoal herringbone jacket, tan
trousers, and new loafers. Some of the black hair dye
had grown out, and his natural reddish-brown hair
could be seen at the nape of his neck.

Newsmen and reporters lined the second-floor corri-
dors as Smitty, smiling tensely, came through the stairwell door from a basement holding cell. Casual, as

though Deputy Henry Booth was not at his back, Smitty paused briefly before Art Meyers, a defense witness. "Good luck," Art said, reaching out his hand.

The courtroom was spacious and new, with bronze reliefs of Lincoln and Washington framing the judge's bench. Schmid sat at the wide glass-topped defense table of light oak, holding 20 blue-bound volumes with gold lettering: *Arizona Revised Statutes Annotated.* Tinney's motions to exclude the press had been denied, and reporters filled seats flanking both sides of a drinking fountain within the railing and to Schmid's right. One newsman's elbow rested on the clerk's desk.

After a few minutes the room slowly started to fill with prospective jurors. Smitty heard a woman whisper: "I thought he was bigger than that. He's really very small, isn't he? Huh, I thought he'd be a lot bigger than that." She sounded disappointed.

"Look at his hands," a man said, leaning toward a heavy-set woman in a flowered dress. "They're small but powerful. You can tell." Smitty took his hands from the table and folded them in his lap. His attorney had advised him to sit quietly and listen attentively.

William Tinney, Schmid's attorney, a deliberate speaker with a slight stutter, which some colleagues insisted won him sympathy, came into the court and sat next to his client. Later Tinney was to tell a friend, "Way back in law school Edward Bennet Williams thought up the rules for practicing criminal law. The four necessary rules are 1—get paid, 2—get a continuance, 3—get another continuance, and 4—never plead guilty."

Then William Schafer III, chosen by the county attorney to prosecute, entered the room through a door to the clerk's office carrying two big manila folders containing the state's case against Charles Schmid.

Finally, the wood panels behind the bench opened and the presiding judge, the Honorable Lee Garrett, an elderly man with slight, birdlike features, his eyes a frosty blue behind rimless glasses, took his seat on the bench.

While the clerk read the roll of ninety-eight prospective jurors, Smitty glanced frequently at the clock. Extra chairs had been brought in to accommodate the overflow of reporters.

It took almost an hour for the last juror to answer, "Here." Judge Garrett then read the formal charges against Schmid.

"The defendant has entered a plea of guilty," the judge said. Smitty seemed dazed, Tinney half-rose from his chair and Schafer blinked curiously at the judge, who sensed the trouble and went on, "Oh, did I say guilty? I meant the defendant is pleading not guilty."

At a recess one reporter discussed the case with several newsmen, and was overheard by some prospective jurors. "The thing about the diary," he said. "Sticking that in there as a motive. They're missing the entire point. The thing about *why* he did it. The question here, which seems to be overlooked, is *why* all these kids knew about the murders and no one said a word."

In the selection of the jurors, the prosecution sought men and women unopposed to the death penalty. Only a few seemed to object to it, and some of these expressed a willingness to allow for it when dealing with "this sort of case." Jurors with any reservations were asked by Schafer: "Even when it deals with the death of a *child*?" and each time Tinney objected to that line of questioning. Jurors with substantial reservations about the death penalty were finally disqualified by the prosecution.

The jury selection moved along slowly. The next day Tinney made a motion for a mistrial when one prospective juror said he could not be impartial in the case because he had two daughters and "the youngest one's name is Wendy." Tinney claimed the answer showed a "hostile attitude and answers to questions that prejudiced Schmid." The motion was denied.

To nearly all the jurors, Tinney's final question was: "Can you promise me that you will base your verdict only on the evidence you hear in court and not on the stuff you have seen or read in the press?"

After exhausting almost the entire ninety-eight-man panel in nearly three full days of examination, a jury was decided upon. Most of those excused said they either couldn't invoke the death penalty or couldn't be locked up for the two or three weeks Judge Garrett had informed them the trial would take.

The jurors included a hardware merchant, a janitor, a copper miner with ten children, the widow of a gas-station operator, a welder's wife, an ex-airline stewardess married to a soft-drink bottling company sales manager, a retired mining engineer, a carpenter's wife, a tavern-owner's wife, the wife of a trailer court manager, and the wife of a loan-company operator.

Only one, a woman, was a lifelong resident of Tucson. Three others had lived in the city approximately twenty years. Some were recent arrivals—from California, Washington, Illinois, Indiana, Iowa, New York, Ohio, West Virginia, and Wisconsin. Most of the twelve were over fifty, three over sixty and only one was below forty. Four men, a widow, and seven middle-aged housewives had testified that they were in favor of the death penalty and "would not hesitate to recommend it."

With the jury dismissed from the courtroom, Tinney submitted a motion to bring in a clinical psychologist to testify that the jurors selected had been subconsciously affected by the pretrial news coverage concerning the case. Glancing at a sheet of yellow legal-pad paper, Tinney said, "Twelve of the jurors have read about the case. Ten have seen it on TV, and six have discussed the case with other people. Seven have heard about it on the radio and one has read about it in *Time* magazine. . . . Now don't get me wrong. I'm not saying the jurors were lying. I know they were telling the truth to the best of their ability. They were not evasive, but I propose to show that subconsciously they had absorbed much of this information. Because of this I am asking the Court to permit me to call Dr.

Roland Tharp, a clinical psychologist at the University of Arizona, and let him testify.

"He will say that even though a person may try to put much information behind him, he cannot really do so because of the subconscious level cranked into the mind at the unconscious level. A person may be as honest as the day is long, but he cannot control what remains in his subconscious mind."

Judge Garrett said he would hear the psychologist's testimony the next day in the absence of the jury.

Eight-thirty the next morning Tinney produced a large cardboard box filled with newspaper clippings, TV and radio tapes, and a bulky roll of posters covered with clippings on the Schmid case. He also submitted tear sheets from the last few editions of the Tucson newspapers, with red and blue marks indicating stories, articles, and photographs relating to the trial.

"These exhibits," Tinney said, "are intended to support my contention that even though the jurors have been honest and upright, they may have erred in saying they had not actually made up their minds about Schmid's guilt or innocence."

When Dr. Tharp took the witness stand he looked over the exhibits, thought over each question carefully and testified "it would be impossible for a juror who has read or seen accounts of the Schmid case to disregard this in reaching a verdict."

After this testimony, Judge Garrett said that psychiatry was a recent and hardly exact science. He spoke of the "study of the mind" as on a par with hypnotism and witchcraft. What Dr. Tharp might say today, Judge Garrett said, he would deny tomorow on the basis of further discoveries made in the interim. Therefore, he denied the motion for a one-year postponement of the trial, concluding: "All of the jurors have stated they will be fair and just in their deliberation."

The bailiff left the room to summon the jury and Smitty wrote on a sheet of yellow paper:

My trial actually begins. It's been such a long time just waiting, I can't believe it's really happening. It's hard to believe what I'm really doing here, but here I am. It was sure nice outside, the air was cold and sort of like crystals but the sun was very bright, for the minute or two I got to see it. I sure wanted to be with Diane. I wonder if she went to the movies the other night and what she saw. I hope I can be with her before Easter anyway. I guess we're about ready to begin. . . .

The jury was seated and William Schafer stood up, consulted a sheet of paper on the table, laid his pencil aside, and turned to the jury. It was nine-thirty.

"Ladies and gentlemen of the jury," Schafer began. "Now is the time that is set aside in each trial for the State, or the Prosecution, and the Defense, if it so desires, to give you an outline of what our evidence will show.

"The story of this case, the murders of Gretchen and Wendy Fritz, Number 15028, will be told by about thirty witnesses, more or less, doctors, police officers, anthropologists, and teen-agers; teen-agers who knew both Wendy and Gretchen Fritz, and who knew the defendant. And when these stories are told, when all this evidence is pieced together, you will see that the State has proved to you two first-degree murders . . . with deliberation, with premeditation; two murders with a motive; two murders to cover up a prior murder. The story of——"

"—If it please the Court," William Tinney said, interrupting the prosecutor. "If counsel could approach the bench."

"You may," Judge Garrett replied.

Out of the jury's hearing, Schafer and Tinney stood before the bench. Tinney said, "If the Court please, on the basis of the County Attorney's opening statement and his comment that he would prove that the motive for the alleged homicide was to cover up for a prior murder, I move for a mistrial and ask at this time to be heard on my argument in support of that. It is highly prejudicial."

"There will be other references to the same thing I will make in the next few minutes," Schafer said.

The judge ruled that Tinney could argue his objection to the motive of a prior murder at the conclusion of Schafer's opening statement without prejudicing his objection. "Is that agreeable?" Judge Garrett asked.

"It is not agreeable," Tinney replied. "No, if that is the Court's decision, that is the Court's decision. I perhaps can reserve my right now to argue any further comments along this line."

Then Schafer resumed his address to the jury: ". . . Case No. 15028 begins in the very early morning hours on November 10, 1965. It was on that morning a number of police officers and one boy got into a car and drove off into the desert off Pontatoc Road. . . ." He told how the skeletons had been found, and how they were identified as Gretchen and Wendy Fritz, "two girls who had disappeared from home on the night of August 16, 1965, when they did not return home from a movie at the Cactus Drive-In." Schafer said, "Now that really is the end of the story of Gretchen and Wendy Fritz.

"The beginning of that story goes back some months before that, actually before they even knew the defendant, Charles Schmid. They met him, at least Gretchen did, sometime in the fall of 1964. But before that you will see the facts that gave rise to this, the circumstances that were mentioned occurred before that, months before that, May 31, 1964.

"You will hear that Gretchen knew, because the defendant told her, that on that night he and John Saunders and Mary French killed a young woman named Alleen Rowe and that he had taken Gretchen Fritz out to where that body was buried east of town in the desert, which was a secret. She kept this secret all during the time she dated Charles Schmid, and she went with Charles Schmid, and this continued for a number of months from the fall when they first met in 1964, through that fall, the winter and into the spring of 1965. . . .

"Shortly after that, however, that relationship began to change. The relationship began to wane. What was once there apparently was not there anymore. It was considerably lessened. It was about this time that Gretchen started to pester and bother the defendant . . . . She called him any number of times . . . sometimes as much as five or six times a day. She was greatly annoyed that he was seen with other girls; that there were gatherings and parties at his house, of the defendant, where other girls attended; Gretchen did not attend any of these parties. She called for him at his house. This pestering and bothering did upset the defendant. He expressed this to a number of his friends. He told that he was tired of it. That he did not like it and that he didn't want to take any more of it, that he did not like the bothering and the pestering. But he told a number of people that he could not stop what was going on because there was something Gretchen Fritz had over him, something that she had that made him do what he did.

"You will hear that he told one of his closest friends, Richard Bruns, that he had killed the Rowe girl, and he had told Gretchen about it, and that Gretchen is holding this against him, and that he cannot do what he wants because of this.

"Then you will hear that in July 1965, shortly before the girls disappeared, the defendant took in two boarders—[William Morgen and his wife Doris] who is a cripple, confined to a wheelchair. She spent a lot of time, and she lived with the defendant at home. Most of her time was spent there.

". . . From the begining of July, that time on to the end of July . . . they lived at Charles Schmid's home. You will hear that during this time a number of friends came over to the house on various occasions and during this time Mr. Schmid expressed [to Mr. Morgen] that he did not like the pestering and bothering. [Mr. Morgen] will tell you that every day Gretchen would call the house, but he did not see Gretchen very often, but he talked to her a number of times on the phone. A number of times she would come over to the house and meet the defendant behind the house back in the alley and a number of times he would go out and apparently meet her.

"And then you will hear that one night when [Mr. Morgen] was sitting with the defendant in the car in front of the house, the defendant told [Mr. Morgen] that Gretchen had stolen a diary of his . . . and that it contained something that would put him in jail for a long time. He told this to Mr. [Morgen] as well as to a few other friends that there was a diary that Gretchen had had that he could not get it back, and that whatever was in it would get him into an awful lot of trouble with the police. To one person he said that whatever was in it would put him in the electric chair.

". . . On this occasion he tells [Mr. Morgen] the story that is in the diary. He told him and he also told this, I believe, to two young teen-agers, who you will see here, that in the diary is the story of his killing a young boy, a sixteen-year-old boy he killed. That this young boy was in an automobile accident with a prior girl friend of Schmid's. The girl was killed, but the boy was unharmed. That after this Mr. Schmid took the boy out to the desert, shot him, killed him, cut off his hands, and buried him. This is what he told [Mr. Morgen]. He also told [Mr. Morgen] this is what Gretchen had against him. And this is why she does what she does.

". . . [Mrs. Morgen] also answered the phone a number of times. She will tell you that Gretchen called five or six times a day, every day, practically . . . and that many times they had arguments on the phone, many arguments about the diary that [Mrs. Morgen] had heard. That the defendant expressed to them a desire to kill Gretchen. He said a couple of times, 'I am going to kill her.' [Mr. Morgen] will describe to you that he used some kind of action with his hands. He told both of them on one occasion that he was going to strangle her, would like to get her neck and strangle her. On another occasion he told [Mr. Morgen] that 'What is in that diary will get me into a whole lot of trouble with the police, and I am going to get that diary. I know there is a way.'

"They moved away at the end of July and they can tell you that shortly before they moved away, Mr. Schmid, the defendant here, told them that sooner or later, within a few days, Gretchen is going to go away she is going to go to Ohio with an aunt, or some statement like that. She is going to live with an aunt. While the [Morgens] are there with the defendant, Gretchen never does leave. [Mrs. Morgen] will tell you that all of a sudden there came a day there were no more phone calls from Gretchen, she was no longer aware of her calls. But Gretchen actually did go away in the month of August, but she went west to California on a vacation with her family, and then she came back from California, which was about August 10th or 11th.

"A day or so after that the defendant comes over to Gretchen's house at night, sometime around nine. Her brother, Robert Fritz, who is sixteen years old, lets him in the back door and once in the door he goes straight to Gretchen's bedroom. The brother listens. He hears them argue. The defendant comes out, after a few minutes, and is followed by Gretchen, who is crying. They go out to the backyard and they argue some more and the brother can't make out the argument. The defendant hits Gretchen and knocks her against the wall. He leaves and he says, 'That's it,' or 'that's the end.'

"This is just one or two days before the girls disappear. You will hear that on the afternoon of the 16th of August, a Monday, the defendant and Gretchen argue again. This time on the phone. And this was a good argument. We will then hear that that evening the Fritz family decide they were going to go to a drive-in. Mr. and Mrs. Fritz went to one drive-in and so far as they knew Gretchen and her sister Wendy were going to go to another drive-in, the Cactus Drive-In. They did leave the house. That is the night the girls disappeared.

"The next day you will hear that there were a number of phone calls which were exchanged between the defendant and some of his teen-age friends, and between Mrs. Fritz and the defendant.

"You will hear that within a number of days after the disappearance of the girls, the defendant told a number of people that the girls were in California, that they were with somebody but he didn't say who, somebody he knew how to contact, only he could do it. He told other people that he had taken the girls to Mexico for a day, and then to California. He told some that he did not know where they were. You will hear one teen-ager say that she called Charles Schmid and talked to him and he had told her that he had seen Wendy and Gretchen just five hours before they disappeared. That he told this girl that Gretchen and Wendy came to him and Gretchen wanted the defendant to marry her. He refused. They argued and they left, and that was the last he saw of them. You will hear that within a week or two weeks after the girls disappeared he took his closest friend, Richard Bruns, to the place where he had hidden the bodies. You will hear at that time that shortly before that he told Richard Bruns that he had killed the girls. He told him that he had killed Gretchen first and then Wendy, and he made a motion with his hands; and then he took them up to Pontatoc and dumped them there, and within that period of two weeks he takes Mr. Bruns out to where the bodies are located and within two months after that, Mr. Bruns, as you have heard, tells the police and initiated the search that I have described to you.

"When you hear all these things and see these witnesses, it will be the only conclusion, that this defendant committed murder in the first degree on Gretchen and Wendy Fritz and there is one penalty. Thank you."

Schafer, head bowed slightly, returned to his table and sat down. The judge looked at Tinney.

"Do you have any legal matters you want to take up now?"

Tinney rose. "I have a legal matter but I would like to make the opening statement, and take that up first."

"You may."

Tinney stood at the end of the defense table, his hands resting on the statute books, and he did not move during his statement, but spoke directly to the body of jurors.

"I think first, we better say, so it is clear right now, that anything that the prosecutor has said or anything that I am going to say, is not evidence. It is only what we think the evidence is going to be and what we think we can prove to you.

"You aren't going to hear any evidence in this case until a witness is sworn by that clerk and that witness walks over and gets in that chair and talks to you. All that our comments are for is to orient you in outline form about the case that we are going to prove to you. It is going to become apparent in a minute that each of us thinks we are going to prove something different to you. A whole lot of small pieces are going to come out in this case. The evidence is going to show a whole lot of small pieces, however, all of the case is not going to be given to you by thirty witnesses, because I have a few witnesses that you will hear from. And all of the case is not in until after you have heard those thirty witnesses. In fact, as the Court will instruct you, you are not to even begin talking about this case between yourselves until after *all* of the evidence is in, or even to decide anything until all of the evidence is in.

"Our case, our case is that Smitty did not kill Gretchen and the child. They argued like kids do. They argued hot and heavy and then ten minutes later they loved. And Gretchen was never afraid of Smitty. And Smitty never threatened Gretchen's life. But somebody did kill Gretchen and the child. Somebody hated Gretchen, and Gretchen was afraid of somebody. And somebody threatened Gretchen's life and somebody knows too much about how the girls died. And somebody fingered Smitty for it. And somebody was Bruns."

The prosecution's first witness was Mrs. Nancy Fritz. She answered Schafer's questions calmly but when asked to identify articles of clothing, she crumpled. "Yes, yes, those are theirs," she said, her breath magnified through the microphone at her throat. Then with a sudden move she turned her face from the shoe boxes containing the articles.

Tinney objected to the prosecutor's insistence on the

identification, and stipulated he would agree that "those particular clothing were the kind of clothing worn by the two sisters." Mrs. Fritz regained her composure and told the Court of the last time she had seen her daughters.

She said of Schmid, "He always acted courteous toward Gretchen in my presence. Gretchen never expressed any fear of Schmid, and she never told me about him saying he murdered someone."

In cross-examination, Tinney questioned her about Bruns, and related the incident of Bruns threatening Gretchen with a gun. "Was Gretchen afraid of Bruns?" Tinney asked.

Mrs. Fritz replied, "I wouldn't say she was afraid of him, but she disliked him."

Following Mrs. Fritz on the stand were a number of witnesses called by Schafer to establish the discovery and identity of the remains found in the desert and the possible cause of death. On the stand, Dr. Louis Hirsch was asked by Schafer about possible neck injuries, and the pathologist said that the remains were "too mummified" to make such a determination.

It was the prosecution's theory that the girls had been strangled with a cord from Schmid's guitar, and a number of witness were presented to try to establish this point. Detectives testified that they found a guitar cord in the desert near the jawbone of one skull, but could not support this finding with a police photograph. A Sears, Roebuck employee said that the cord "fit" Smitty's guitar, and added, "It's a very popular model." A man from a pawnshop said that the guitar had been pawned there on July 20 by the defendant, but he didn't know if the cord was with the guitar on that date. The detective who retrieved the guitar from the pawnshop testified that he turned the guitar and a guitar cord over to the City County Crime Lab, where Captain Kempe had been unable to determine if the cord "found at the scene" had been the cord used on Schmid's guitar. Under cross-examination, the captain acknowledged that the cord could have fit a number of guitars, including Schmid's.

Despite the ambiguity over the guitar cord, the Tucson newspapers summed the testimony in headlines: "Guitar Cord Murder Weapon," and "Strangled By Guitar Cord."

The next day the prosecution called Irma Jean Kolt's mother, who testified that during the period her husband had worked with Smitty in the upholstery business she had overheard a telephone conversation between Smitty and Gretchen. "When he hung up," Mrs. Kolt said, almost snapping at her, "he said, 'I'm going to kill that bitch.'"

Mrs. Kolt said Gretchen called Smitty two or three times a day and that "He told me, 'I wish she'd get off my back—disappear—get lost—quit hounding me.'" She said the defendant told her Gretchen was holding something over his head, but that she didn't know what it was.

Tinney was able to bring out that Mrs. Kolt did not think Smitty was making a real threat. "You didn't think about calling up the police," Tinney asked, "to say there was going to be a homicide?"

"No, sir," Mrs. Kolt replied.

Her daughter Irma Jean took the stand, her hair combed so it practically covered one eye. About the diary, she testified: "I asked him why he did everything Gretchen said, why he jumped every time she asked for something. . . . Smitty said Gretchen had stolen a diary from his house and that the diary contained information about a guy he had killed, cut off his hands and buried, in the east." She said that Smitty had further told her, "He hated Gretchen and wished she'd stop bothering him."

Tinney asked her if she'd considered telling the police about the diary. Irma Jean replied, "I just didn't think it was true. I just let it slide by." Then she smiled at Smitty from the witness stand and as she passed the defense table she whispered to Smitty, "How are you?"

Shirley and Kitty Bates both testified that they had heard Smitty tell Irma Jean about the diary. Her eyes darting nervously about the courtroom, Shirley said she had visited Smitty's house a number of times during the summer and had heard Smitty express dislike for Gretchen.

Kitty burst into tears when her eyes met Smitty's. "I can't look at him," she sobbed.

Robert Fritz testified to the argument between Gretchen and Smitty outside the Fritz home a few days before Gretchen disappeared. He said Schmid pushed her against a wall, and "Gretchen fell down crying,"

Robert recalled. "He said, 'That's it!' and she said, 'Don't,' or something like that."

The jury was told how Schmid had asked Charles Stenz to arrange to meet Gretchen in the park, so that Schmid would have an excuse to break off their relationship. Stenz said Schmid was hiding in the bushes. "He came out and slapped her down. She got up and started crying." Stenz also recalled that Smitty had said, ". . . Sooner or later I am going to kill that bitch," and added that he did not think this was uttered "in a joking manner."

On Monday morning, February 21, the prosecution called John Saunders to the witness stand. When Schafer asked John his name, he replied: "I refuse to answer the question on the ground that it may tend to incriminate me under the laws of Arizona and the United States."

Saunders gave the same reply to two more questions until Tinney objected to further questions, "on the ground that these kind of answers are prejudicial in front of the jury." Judge Garrett had the jury removed from the courtroom and Tinney moved for a mistrial, arguing that "Saunders should not have been placed on the stand if it was known that he would answer in the manner he did. The answers could cast a question in the mind of the jury about what he might say—and cause the jury to begin speculating." The prosecution withdrew Saunders and Tinney's motion was denied.

After a short recess, the next witness called was Mary French. She entered the courtroom apprehensively, shoulders slumped. Her hair was fluffed out in a bouffant style but there was little color in her face. She wore a camel sweater and a tan skirt. After a few routine questions, Tinney objected to her testifying, because she could not have knowledge of the murder of the Fritz sisters, since she was not in Tucson at the time of their death and was appearing solely to testify to another crime (for which there was no corpus delicti), "because it might prove a motive in this case." Tinney's objection was overruled.

Mary spoke without a break in her deadpan composure, although she was asked several times to "speak up." Her account of the murder of Alleen Rowe, delivered in an amplified monotone, seemed to hypnotize the crowd of spectators filling the extra chairs and standing within the courtroom.

After Schafer's direct examination, in which there was no mention of Gretchen or Wendy Fritz, Tinney, in his cross-examination, made it plain that Mary had not seen the actual murder of Alleen Rowe, and that she had not tried to warn Alleen that she was in danger, even though Schmid had told her he intended to kill Alleen. Tinney also tried to discredit Mary's motive for testifying by asking her about the child she told Smitty she was going to have. She admitted that she had not given birth.

"After your staying with Charlie as husband and wife for that period of time, did you get angry with him?" Tinney asked.

"Yes," Mary replied.

"Over another girl?"

"Yes."

"And was that other girl Gretchen or some other girl?"

"Gretchen."

Paul Graff was called, as a hostile witness. He had been brought from New Orleans to testify for the prosecution, although the police there had told him he did not have to return to Tucson as a witness. Outside the courtroom, Paul said that Chief Garmire had warned him that if he did not testify for the state, there would be a warrant issued for his arrest. "I was told this," Paul says, "and if I didn't say exactly what they wanted me to say, I'd be held and questioned in regards to *my* part in the thing."

On the stand, Paul said he had lived at Schmid's house for a couple of weeks the preceding September. Smitty had told him about killing a girl in the desert, and that Saunders and Mary French were with him at the time of the killing. Paul said he discounted the story. "He asked me to go out and see the grave, almost in a joking manner. I didn't go."

Asked by Schafer if Schmid told him where the girl was buried, Paul said, "He just made a vague reference to an old drinking spot."

Schmid's affair with Gretchen was "a stormy one," Paul admitted. "One time he would tell me he was madly in love with her, then that they had an argument, and again that he was in love with her." Paul said he moved out of Smitty's house following a disagreement. "Smitty got very emotional, I hadn't seen him get that way before. He smashed his fist into a wall and said God was punishing him."

Tinney brought out in cross-examination, over Schafer's objections, the bad feelings between Gretchen and Bruns. Paul said that Bruns told him he "detested —hated—liked to throttle—kill," Gretchen because she had "blackballed him at high school socially."

Paul said he had never heard of a diary until a few weeks before when he was questioned by the police. He said that Dupnik, having come to New Orleans, told him the police had pages of this diary. But Paul said, "I never saw the pages or had heard of a diary up to that time."

After he left the witness stand, Paul was approached by newsmen in the corridor who barraged him with questions. He stared at them blandly for a moment, then said, "I utterly despise Tucson, its police, the Tucson newspapers and you. I hope I never come here again. All I want to do is get out of this town. You had your say in 1957." He left Tucson on a Greyhound bus the following morning.

Bill Morgen, summoned by the prosecution, entered the courtroom in rumpled pants and soiled checkered shirt. His wife, Doris, slumped in her wheelchair, hair untidy, waited in the hallway to testify after her husband.

"Schmid said he'd been in love with this girl," Bill Morgen recalled from the witness stand, "and this girl and this guy got involved in an auto accident and the girl was killed, so he took this guy out in the desert, the guy begged for his life, but he said he shot him anyway and cut off his hands." Morgen said Schmid had told him Gretchen had stolen the diary, and now had enough on Schmid to send him to the electric chair. "I didn't believe Schmid was capable of a murder," but he quoted Schmid as saying, "I'd like to kill that bitch. I'd like to twist her pretty little neck."

Mrs. Morgen, testifying from her wheelchair, said when Schmid told her about the diary, she said "Oh, no, Smitty, you're kidding. And he said 'No, I'm serious.'" Later he told her, "There has got to be a way to get it back. I'm making plans now."

About a week before they left his house, she said, "Smitty rushed into the house and closed windows and pulled down the blinds. He was shaking all over . . . looked real pale. I asked him what was wrong and he said 'The cops are coming to get me—Gretchen has turned me in.'" On another occasion he told her Gretchen was returning the diary and giving him some money. "He had just talked to her on the phone and seemed real happy."

One night, Smitty came home dirty and said Gretchen had left him out in the desert and he'd had to walk back. That was when he said, "I'm going to kill her when I get my hands on her." Like the other witnesses, Mrs. Morgen had not taken Schmid's threats seriously.

Wednesday morning, February 23, Richie Bruns arrived at Superior Court. He wore tight black Continental slacks, high-heeled Beatle boots, and his hair was heaped up in a pompadour and combed straight back on the sides. He walked casually into the court-room wearing a pair of purple wrap-around sunglasses, which he removed as he took the witness stand. During the lengthy testimony that followed, he looked at Smitty frequently, evenly. Richie could recall nothing by calendar dates, only by incidents surrounding the dates in question.

He said that Smitty had told him about the killing of Alleen Rowe, and recounted some of the details of that conversation, such as the hunting trip with Saunders when Smitty had "stuck a stick in the ground to see how she smelled after she had been there so long."

Richie testified as to the off-again on-again relation-ship between Smitty and Gretchen. He told of Smitty's increasing anger, of his actions shortly before Gretchen disappeared, and of Smitty's confessing the murder to him. He talked about the incident with the Tucson Mafia and then of accompanying Smitty to try and bury the bodies of the Fritz girls. As they went back to the car that night Smitty told him, "You are in it as deep as I am now."

Under extensive cross-examination, Tinney brought out Bruns's ill-feelings toward Gretchen, despite Schafer's repeated objections. But he was unable to show that Bruns had done more than talk against Gretchen. And Tinney was unable to shake Richie's basic story—that Smitty had told him he had killed the Fritz sisters and had taken him to the graves.

Tinney asked, "After you got up in Ohio did it concern you that your handkerchief was back at the grave site?"

"No," Richie replied.

"Did it concern you that perhaps your prints might be on Gretchen's shoes?"

Richie said, "No."

"Did it concern you that perhaps your prints were on the tennis shoe?"

"No."

"Did it concern you that your prints might be on Gretchen's shoe?"

"No."

Asked if he'd ever discussed putting the bodies on Darlene Kirk's front door, Richie replied that he had. "I came over and he [Smitty] asked me how I was getting along with [Darlene]. I said I wasn't getting along too good. He said maybe we ought to get Gretchen and put a noose around her neck and put her on the front porch, and ring the doorbell and that would bring her around."

"And Smitty said that?" Tinney asked.

"Yes."

Gloria Andrews was among the remaining teen-agers waiting to testify for the prosecution. Oddly, testimony that was basically confusing became, according to the press, the "most damning evidence."

Wearing a furry white sweater, with her bleached hair framing her colorless face, Gloria testified that she had gone to Smitty's house for a party on the night of

August 16, and that "Not long after I got to the house there was a phone call and Smitty told Paul to answer it. Paul told Smitty it was Gretchen, and that she wanted to meet him and if he didn't come, that she'd tell her father."

According to Gloria, Smitty "started walking into the bedroom and called Paul to come with him, and I heard Smitty say 'I'm going to get that bitch if it's the last thing I do.' Then Smity said he was going to see Gretchen."

Gloria testified that Smitty and Paul left the house, Smitty carrying an old black briefcase. They returned between one and one-thirty in the morning.

"I was the only one there," Gloria said. "As they approached, I heard Smitty say 'You'd better shut up, [Mike] and the rest might still be there.'" As they came into the house Paul said that he "wasn't in it and wasn't going to get in it."

Schafer asked Gloria to describe Schmid's appearance at that time. She said, "He was pretty messed up. His hair was down all over his face, he was dusty and raggedy looking, he looked scared, he looked like something was wrong with him." Paul left the house minutes later, Gloria said, and took two large butcher knives with him. The next day she received a call from Schmid and he said the Fritz girls were missing and, "He said now he could go out with anyone he wanted to."

Tinney's cross-examination established that Gloria had trouble remembering things. Asked when she first attended one of Smitty's parties, she said around the first of August, but admitted she was uncertain who was there. Tinney pressed for this information, and Gloria replied, "I don't know who all was there because I got drunk."

"Because you were drunk?" Tinney echoed.

"Yes, and I don't know who all was there," Gloria repeated. The calm she had sustained through Schafer's questioning was starting to wear thin under Tinney's probing. He asked for further details on the party. Gloria said she had been brought to the party early, between five and seven by a boy named Gerry Wells. When Tinney asked her what time she left. Gloria replied, "Oh . . . oh, that night we stayed all night."

Tinney continued to ask about this party and found that Gloria, her sister Martha (then fifteen), and another girl stayed all night, but Gloria wasn't sure whether Gerry stayed. Then Tinney asked about another party, two weeks after the Fritz girls disappeared. This time Gloria said Jimmy Scott had brought her to the party and she supplied the names of others who had been there.

"What time did you get to that party?" Tinney asked.

After a pause, Gloria replied, "I don't remember."

"Did you have anything to drink that night?"

"I don't know."

"Did you get drunk that night?"

"No."

"Did you stay all night?"

"No."

"What time did you go home that night?"

Gloria sat staring blankly at Tinney. He said, "Was your answer that you don't know again?"

She didn't reply. Her shoulders started to shake and she began to cry.

"Who took you home?" Tinney repeated.

"I guess it was [Jimmy]."

"I don't want a guess," Tinney demanded. "Who?"

Gloria started to sob. She tried to speak but couldn't. Judge Garrett interrupted the proceedings as Gloria mumbled something that sounded as if she said Jimmy Scott had "promised" to take her home.

Finally, she gained control of herself and Tinney again asked whether Jimmy had indeed taken her home from Smitty's. "I don't remember," Gloria replied.

Tinney moved his line of questioning to the night of August 16, but the only admission he could gain from Gloria was that she had been in Smitty's house during the time the Fritz girls were killed and had not seen or heard any violence. This contradicted the story Bruns claimed he had heard from Smitty, that the girls had been murdered in the living room.

Gloria Andrews left the courtroom in tears. She stood trembling in the corridor; there was no one to meet her. A photographer aimed his camera and she covered her face with her sweater, then ran downstairs and outside into the crowd that lined the street to watch the annual Fiesta de los Vaqueros parade.

Martha, Gloria's younger sister, nervously gripping the arms of the witness chair, testified that she had attended several parties at Schmid's house that summer. But she didn't go to the house on the night of August 16.

Several other witnesses added a few minor details and then the prosecution closed its case. Tinney made a series of motions for a direct acquittal, for a reduction of charges, for striking certain testimony, and a motion for mistrial based on the testimony concerning the deaths of Alleen Rowe and the unnamed boy buried in the desert, "the boy with his hands cut off." He argued that the state had not proven a corpus delicti in either case. "I don't think testimony about these things was necessary . . . and obviously it was prejudicial," Tinney said. He also argued that the state produced no evidence by any coroner, pathologist, or eyewitness, and no confession as to how the girls actually died.

In denying Tinney's motions, Judge Garrett said the evidence "is not weak from a legal standpoint at this time," and he would leave the degree of murder to be determined by the jury.

The defense started by calling a series of witnesses testifying to the "stream of hostility" between Bruns and Gretchen. Jimmy Scott, sixteen, confirmed the threats made by Bruns and the hostility Bruns had displayed toward Gretchen. But under cross-examination by Schafer, Scott disclosed that he had discussed plans to "get Bruns for telling the police that Smitty had murdered Gretchen and Wendy."

Schafer asked, "Did you talk of shooting him?"

"Yes," Scott replied.

Referring to Ronald Baines, the next witness scheduled to be called by the defense, Schafer asked Scott: "Was mention made of using the guns [Baines] had?"

"Yes."

"One of the shotguns could be used to get Bruns?"

"Yes," Scott answered. When Schafer asked whether he had been present at a party in August, when Smitty received a phone call from Gretchen, Scott said that he had, and the call had enraged Smitty. "He was shouting," Scott testified, "said he would kill her."

On the witness stand, Ronald Baines claimed he had heard Bruns say that he'd "like to kill Gretchen and was going to kill her. Bruns said that he didn't think Gretchen was good enough for Smitty." That same evening, he said he'd seen Bruns "waving around a chrome-plated pistol."

Under cross-examination, Baines admitted he disliked Bruns intensely. "Isn't it true that Bruns idolized the defendant?" Schafer asked.

"Yes, sir," Baines replied.

"And isn't it true that Bruns dressed like him?"

"Yes sir."

"And you did too, dress like the defendant?"

"Sometimes," Baines said, red-faced, nervous, uncertain of what he was saying. Schafer had weakened the point of Bruns's threats to kill Gretchen by disclosing the plans the group had made to kill Bruns. A shot-gun, to the jury, seemed a more deadly weapon than a chrome-plated pistol.

The defense had established through the testimony of Scott and Jack Spiers, sixteen, that Paul Graff had not been present at the party in August that Gloria Andrews had attended. The party Gloria had attended, Spiers testified, had occurred in September. He added that Gloria was "quite drunk" that night, and that he did not see Paul at any of Schmid's parties in August.

A number of young girls also testified to Bruns's feelings against Gretchen. One was Darlene Kirk. But when Tinney tried to bring out the threats Bruns had made against Darlene and her family, Schafer objected and Judge Garrett ruled that "Bruns is not on trial here. Whether Miss [Kirk] was afraid of Bruns is not material."

When Schmid heard this ruling he threw down a ball-point pen in disgust. "Stop that," Tinney told him, and Schmid folded his hands in his lap.

Tinney called Charles Schmid, Sr.

Middle-aged, slightly stoop-shouldered, wearing a loose-fitting green suit and horn-rimmed glasses, Mr. Schmid took the stand. He avoided Smitty's intent gaze and addressed his answers to the jury.

He said his son, Charlie, sometimes helped out at the nursing home and played his guitar at local nightclubs. Charlie received an allowance of approximately $300 per month, he said, and he and his wife let Charlie move into the little house next door and knew about the parties but never interfered.

Mr. Schmid had not see his son on the night of August 16, but said his wife telephoned there around 10:30 to get them to quiet down. At that time, he recalled, Charlie was in his house.

Charles, Sr., answered in a straightforward manner but in one way his testimony virtually abolished the alibi entered earlier in the trial by Tinney, who said he had obtained information that Schmid was with another couple, or his parents, on the night of August 16.

Court was adjourned until Monday morning. That night, Friday, February 25, from his cell in Pima County Jail, Smitty wrote to Diane:

It's strange but for the first time I've actually come to the realization that I'm being framed and that in a few weeks time I'll be dead. I don't really think we'll win anymore. The witnesses we have all did their best to tell the truth, but I guess it's not enough. Gloria and Martha lied as did Richie, but I guess you know that by now. If it wasn't for all the bad publicity, maybe I'd of had a chance, but I was convicted before the case was ever tried. I guess everyone had their revenge for me being nice to them. The press *never gave me* a chance. I guess they were paid off. Ronnie Baines told how the cops coerced him, but I doubt if anyone believed him. They won't allow any of the evidence against Richie in. Some of my witnesses won't testify. I guess there is nothing else to do but let them finish what they started. It would be too late to do anything without causing a lot of red faces.

"Face it, honey, they're big wheels and they can't afford to admit to defeats. It shouldn't bother them to kill me because I'm nobody to them. They've twisted and distorted the truth *so* bad I'm even mixed up. I'm not really scared to die, but I wish we could of had more time together. We could have been so happy. I guess that's fate tho! Well, maybe they have guitars in heaven.

During the trial, no witness was to reveal as much composure or self-assurance as Mrs. Katharine Schmid. On Monday, February 28, she took the stand to try to provide an alibi for Smitty on the night of August 16. She appeared calm, a stout well-built woman, wearing glasses, black round-neck silk dress, a six-strand pearl necklace, little pearl earrings, and a close-fitting hairdo.

She repeated what her husband had already said, that she had called her son on the phone the night of August 16 "and told him to turn down the music so as not to create a disturbance." About ten minutes later, she said, "Charlie came over to the house and said he'd be more quiet. He sat down on the floor, ate pizza with us, and watched television for a while. And then he went home."

Paul had not been at Smitty's house during the entire month of August 1965, Mrs. Schmid testified. She was sure because a boy named Bobby Garcia had been staying there at the time. She said she had carried three meals over to the little house for them. (Tinney had planned to call Bobby Garcia as a witness. Garcia was in the courtroom on Monday morning, but when his name was called he could not be found.)

The guitar cord the state had introduced in evidence as being found near the Fritz girls' bodies was black. Mrs. Schmid testified that "all of Charlie's guitar cords were gray."

Even under strong cross-examination, Katharine Schmid had a sharp answer for practically every question. Smitty hunched forward in his seat when Schafer asked Mrs. Schmid, "Is he your son?"

She said, "He has been my son since he was one day old. He is my son by choice." Mrs. Schmid had never questioned him about what he did with his $300 allowance, and she paid his bills for him. She also served him meals in the little house and kept it clean for him.

"Did he have a regular job?" Schafer asked.

"Well, he mowed the lawn sometimes and was always available to do anything I wanted," Mrs. Schmid replied. "He would do anything I asked." But she admitted he had no regular duties.

"How many parties were held in your son's house in July and August of last year?" Schafer inquired.

"Four or five."

"Were you aware of the parties?"

"Yes."

"Were you aware of the ages of the girls who attended them?"

"Some of them."

"But you never asked your son about them?"

"I did not."

Schafer also asked Mrs. Schmid about Gretchen Fritz. Did Mrs. Schmid like her?

"Personally, no," she replied. "I did not like Gretchen because of the reputation she had."

"Did you ever talk to your son about her reputation?"

"I did not. I never discussed Gretchen with anybody."

"Was his [Smitty's] relationship with Gretchen good?" Schafer asked.

"The same as any other so-called romance."

"Did you ever see Gretchen?"

"I did not."

Schafer also inquired about Smitty's habits of dress. "How tall are you?" he asked Mrs. Schmid.

"About five foot five inches."

"How tall is Charlie?"

"About the same height."

"Did you know he wore lifts in his boots and practiced walking in them?"

"He wore lifts in his boots to make himself three inches taller."

"Did he practice walking with these things in his boots?"

After a pause, she replied, "Yes."

Tinney called only two further witnesses. One, Honey Prince, seventeen, stated that the party Gloria Andrews had testified about as occurring on August 16 had actually taken place on September 8. Honey knew because she kept a diary about such activities. The second witness, Art Meyer, said that he'd been with Bruns until 6:30 on August 16, but not after that. Bruns had testified he'd spent most of that evening with Meyer.

The following day, March 1, both the prosecution and defense made their final arguments and gave the case to the jury. Schafer explained to the jurors that under Arizona law first-degree murder was "the unlawful killing of a human being with malice aforethought." He summarized all the occasions on which Schmid had threatened to do away with Gretchen. "You will remember," Schafer said, "that, from Charles Stenz on to all the other witnesses, we showed you, time and time again, statements by the defendant, not in jest, not in a joking manner, [but] serious, when he was mad, when he was hot mad. . . ." Schafer defined the threats to kill Gretchen as "express malice aforethought, a deliberate intention to take away a human life." After defining "implied malice aforethought," Schafter said, "What else but an abandoned and malignant heart . . . dumped the bodies unceremoniously out on the desert ground . . . what else but an abandoned and malignant heart would brag about what happened? What else but an abandoned and malignant heart would kill these girls to cover up a prior murder, the prior murder being that of Alleen Rowe of which you have any number of references to."

Reviewing the testimony, Schafer admitted how heavily the state's case rested on Bruns's testimony. He said, "If you believe Mr. Bruns, there has been a confession in this case. This is all the state need prove to you. We have proved the crime, the unlawful killing. . . . There is a complete and absolute confession by the defendant to Mr. Bruns. If you believe this, the state needs go no further."

Schafer said that if Bruns had been lying he would have made up a much tighter story, one "that would have left you with no doubt in your minds whatever. He could have made up a story as to exactly how it was done." But Bruns's story, Schafer said, had enough small inconsistencies to bear the mark of truth.

After a lengthy review of the testimony, Schafer concluded with a plea for the jury to do its duty. He said they had a decision to make which "no one enjoys making."

"Capital punishment is the most powerful deterrent known to the law," Schafer said, "and in some cases it is the only just result. The punishment must fit the crime. When it does not, the punishment is of no use." In some cases, he said, the jury might find there were circumstances which would militate against the imposition of the death penalty. But, he continued, "There is nothing in this case that we, as human beings, can sympathize with or understand. . . . There is callousness

. . . indifference . . . inhumanity. A killing because of a prior killing does not identify it with anyone. There is no mercy in this case whatsoever. Whatever mercy existed, died in that far-off plot of ground on Pontatoc Road on August 16th."

In concluding his summation, Schafer said, "This man has forfeited any rights that he would have. This man has forfeited his right to walk among us. Your verdict and judgment is death. Thank you."

Tinney, speaking slowly, denied that the state had proved anything. In his closing remarks, he said the prosecution's case left "many whys, wheres, mistakes, and exaggerations," the trial was only an approximation and "the fragile web of circumstantial evidence is only a theory."

Tinney said, "I have a theory too, and that is that Bruns did it and not Schmid." Everyone knew Bruns hated Gretchen, he reminded the jury. "Where was Bruns on the night of August 16?"

Gloria Andrews' testimony he disputed, not by saying she lied but merely by the fact that she was mistaken about the date. The party she thought had taken place in mid-August actually was sometime in September.

Calling for logic and fairness from the jurors, Tinney stood by Schmid's side and said, "I do not deny that there were fights between the defendant and Gretchen and stupid acts. But we do deny murder. Our plea to murder is not guilty."

After a rebuttal by Schafer, Judge Garrett's charge

was brief, saying that they could either find Schmid guilty of murder and recommend the death sentence, find him guilty with a sentence of life imprisonment, or find him innocent. He told them they could convict on circumstantial evidence, but that "If you have a reasonable doubt whether or not the defendant was present at the time the crime was committed, he is entitled to an acquittal."

At 2:15 that afternoon, the jurors walked single file from the courtroom and into the jury room. Tinney gathered his papers, shook Schmid's hand and said, "Charlie, good luck."

In the clerk's office, Judge Garrett told a newsman, "The evidence is circumstantial, but it is for the jury to decide."

The dozens of newsmen and writers for national publications left the court, expecting a long vigil, and except for the clerk gathering exhibits to be taken to the jury room if necessary, the courtroom had emptied by two-thirty. In the corridor, a TV news director said, "It'll be one, maybe two days—they'll bring in an acquittal." The other reporters were waiting near the jury room, discussing which one would remain after midnight when the jury would be taken to the hotel and locked up for the night.

The secretary in Judge Garrett's office said, "The possibility of an early verdict in such a complex case seems remote."

Sitting together on one long Naugahyde sofa, Mr. and

Mrs. Schmid, Diane, and her mother remained in the hallway. "We're going to stick around here," Mr. Schmid told a reporter, "at least for a little while."

At 3:15 the jurors asked for refreshments—Coke, some coffee. It was supplied by one of the bailiffs. Another hour and ten minutes passed. The buzzer from the jury room was sounded again and the bailiff stuck his head into the opened door, then, retreating quickly and closing the door, he said, "They've got a verdict!"

Schafer could not be located. Deputy County Attorney Healy said, "He's on his way home. No one expected a verdict so soon. I'll take it for him."

"Better have them bring Smitty back up here," the bailiff said, "before they take him to jail for the night."

Quickly the courtroom began to fill. There were more spectators now, more newsmen, more than the court could contain. They pushed together in front of the courtroom door. Katharine Schmid waited in the corridor, deciding not to enter the courtroom with Charles, Sr., and Diane.

Tinney walked into the courtroom with a grim, set expression. Smitty was escorted in by Deputy Booth and sat at the defense table, his arms folded, breathing hard. The jury had deliberated two hours and ten minutes when they filed back into the jury box. Finally, Judge Garrett took his seat on the bench.

"Members of the jury have you reached a verdict?" he intoned.

"We have, Your Honor," answered the foreman, hand-ing two slips of paper to the bailiff. The clerk of the court then read them in a quavering voice.

"In the case of the State of Arizona versus Charles Howard Schmid, Jr., we find the defendant guilty and set the penalty at death."

Diane let out a cry and started sobbing uncontrolably. Smitty did not move. Tinney leaned back and blinked several times. Deputy Attorney Healy smiled to himself. The jurors were staring ahead blankly. Smitty waved for his wife to be quiet, but everyone else in the courtroom seemed to be buzzing, blotting out the clerk's reading of the second verdict, that in the murder of Wendy Fritz, guilty, penalty of death. But no one heard it.

Tinney rose and asked that the jury be polled individually, and as they were polled Smitty rocked back and forth, looked at the reporters, the court officials and the clerk, who was reading the roll. Each juror confirmed his verdict, then Tinney requested permission to question the jurors about whether they had been influenced by information they had received outside the courtroom. Garrett denied this, saying: "I've never heard of such a motion before."

The judge thanked the jury and dismissed the jurors, having forgotten to set the time for sentencing. Court was not officially adjourned. Then Diane jumped up in a burst of sobs, climbed the railing separating the spectators from the court, and used a chair as a rung to reach her convicted husband. A newsman grabbed up his camera before she could step on it.

"Smitty! Oh, Smitty!" she cried in his arms.

"It's OK, honey," he said in a half-whisper, "It's OK." At that a cameraman aimed his camera to snap a picture. While Diane was being ushered behind the railing, Judge Garrett's voice rose sharply above the excitement.

"This hasn't been a show!" he said. "You people here would like to make it a show!" Then he snapped to the nearest newsman, pointing threateningly, "Did you take a picture?"

"No, Your Honor," the reporter said.

"Well, you be careful or one of you may wind up in jail. It's not been easy to be lenient with the press in this case. I'll put the first man in jail that takes a picture!"

Tinney then reminded the judge that he had not set the time for sentencing. Judge Garrett restored order to the chaotic courtroom and set the time at March 11, 1966, at nine A.M.

"To avoid another outburst like that," Tinney said, "I ask that Schmid be removed from the court while it is still in session, Your Honor."

"Granted," the judge said and as Deputy Booth led young Schmid away from the defense table, Diane reached out her hand and Smitty squeezed it for a moment before Booth handcuffed his hands behind his back.

"Well, Henry," Smitty said to the deputy, "that's the way it goes." He was escorted out into the hall, past his weeping mother and through the stairwell door to be taken to a car waiting downstairs.

The courtroom cleared, with Diane following Schmid, Sr., through the spectators. Mrs. Lynch was behind her, grasping the girl's arms. Flashbulbs popped, and Schmid, Sr., covered his face with a newspaper.

"Any comment? Any comment?" the reporters entreated. Smitty's father muttered, "We will stand by our son." Diane's mother, trying to protect her, screamed, "Go away, you vultures! You've seen it all, got what you wanted, now go away!"

Outside, Tinney was asked if he planned to appeal. He replied, "I'm going home to dinner. I don't know about you but I'm going home to my wife and family."

The jury foreman was more cooperative. He said, "No particular piece of evidence stood out in our minds. We considered the case as a whole picture. After I was elected foreman we waited about five minutes in silence before we began discussing anything. Then anyone who had anything to say said it, and we let the few members who hadn't spoken think it over for themselves." All the jurors, he continued, "especially the women, were very deliberate when they expressed their views. I personally was a bit surprised to find so much agreement. On the death penalty, on the first and second ballot, two jurors withheld their votes. But there was no argument against the death penalty and after discussion we voted again and reached a decision." It took only one ballot to convict Schmid. But a second was taken to verify, he added. Three ballots were passed before the jury voted unanimously for the death penalty, and this, the foreman said, was accomplished within the first thirty minutes of the time the jury entered the jury room.

Schafer said the verdict was "the quickest ever that I can recall involving the death penalty."

Part 5

THAT EVENING OF March 1st, sitting on the edge of his cot in Cell 14, one leg crossed and the blue-lined writing pad on his knee, Smitty wrote:

The mockery of justice finally completed its cycle and the distortion of truth riddled reality to form a clause of *guilty*. But I expected to lose, any of the fanatical contributions that led to my conviction were deeply embedded in the jurors' minds before any presentation of evidence . . . and the news media groveled in squeamish delight over the anticipation of the verdict.

The hungry cyclopean vultures forever aiming their one eye in my direction. . . . Ultimately and undoubtedly the decision will be reversed and the final revenge will be mine—but alas, revenge is sickening. As I contemplate the future, my mind probes the depths of this solitude in search of a rationalization for this incredible insanity that constantly haunts me, taunting me with thoughts of destruction and the ultimate death they hope to deliver me.

The disappointment was not too harsh as I was rather pessimistic of the outcome. . . . My companionship with Death which will surely be my companion and enemy for a multitude of days, will not conquer me. I will occasionally enjoy the duels with Death and his Associates, and hope my instinctive intrepidness will name me as the victor.

I've considered the remote possibility that my appeal will be rejected and death would be the next progression. At this time, as I shut my eyes and visualize the process of dying, I anticipate a new adventure instead of fear. Naturally, I hate to relinquish my physical existence at this time, but destiny pursues other channels and rivers and I am merely the life-blood of their existence to flow in endless pursuit of its whim.

Schmid continued making entries in his notebook while Tinney began the complicated series of legal maneuvers to appeal the verdict. Tinney contacted the law offices of attorney F. Lee Bailey in Boston, requesting an outline of Bailey's appeal for Dr. Sam

Sheppard, based on "pretrial publicity," upon which Tinney would base the appeal for Schmid.

Schmid wrote:

Today's events poisoned my soul with such fury and insurgent uprisings I actually felt nausea.

As the fires of hell burn perpetually so does the wildness and uninhibited thoughts of my mind. Eternally the primitiveness of my anger roars within the depths of my subconscious to devour my reasoning power. . . . The words and thoughts I transpire come in a rapid staccato from some unknown source below the thoughts of my subconscious. Each conformation of thought that flows from my untapped reservoir is not premeditated, but a hereditary response prompted by the same fury that serves as a guidepost for my actions. . . .

Will life completely banish me, and my identity become so left behind no amount of speed will ever let me surpass it again? I'm so afraid this incredible raw wildness that refuses to lie dormant has driven me down a one-way road of recklessness, completely devoid of detours.

During this time, a journalist who had closely followed the trial gained an interview with a nineteen-year-old boy who claimed to have been a friend of Smitty's, and who had attended some parties on East Adams following the disappearance of the Fritz girls.

The boy, at the time of the interview, was staying in New Mexico as a fugitive from a stolen-car incident in Arizona. He said that on one occasion Smitty had told him how he killed the sisters.

"I don't know why Smitty did it exactly except he said he choked them with his hands. Gretchen's sister was watching TV and he killed Gretchen in the bedroom, then came out and choked the sister. He said Gretchen was making noises and he went back and put her in the living room, and choked her again. He said he choked the sister twice too, even though he knew she was dead the first time. He said he pissed a little in his pants and then sat on the front—the concrete step there—for a while until he got to thinking that he would take the bodies out of the house. He said he dropped them off up in the desert and didn't think about covering them over or hiding them."

The boy also said he had read about the trial and believed Schmid could have "beaten it" with a better lawyer.

In Tucson, Tinney had already made a number of motions for delay of the Rowe trial, because of the unfavorable publicity Schmid had received. Appearing before Judge Mary Ann Richey, Tinney requested a delay of at least five months, saying "We need time for the public to read about other crimes and headlines. We just got through with a trial which had as much publicity as a trial could have. Is it fair to have a trial of this man starting next Tuesday?"

Opposing the motion, Schafer said, "The more time that elapses, the more difficult it will be to find witnesses."

Judge Richey granted a delay, saying: "What bothers me is that in the Fritz murder trial much testimony pertaining to the Rowe case was admitted into evidence and this testimony received about as much coverage as the Fritz case. . . . I think it would be impossible to get a fair and impartial jury at this time. For these two reasons: publicity and the sworn testimony of the Rowe case already made public in the Fritz trial, I am ordering the trial continued to October 4, 1966."

Tinney also attempted to have sentencing postponed in the Fritz conviction, but after one delay Schmid was brought before Judge Garrett in Division II on March 25, 1966. Additional motions to postpone the sentencing were submitted by Tinney, but were rejected by Judge Garrett, who then asked if there were any reason why he should not then pronounce sentence.

Schmid, standing before the bench, stunned the entire courtroom, including his attorney, by bursting out: "I have a reason Your Honor—I demand that I have a sodium pentothal test to prove that I am innocent of these crimes." He continued in an excited voice, saying that his conviction resulted from "the perpetration of a fraud by the police and the County Attorney's office— my conviction was a mockery of justice—the pretrial publicity did nothing but condemn me, condemn me, condemn me!"

Judge Garret replied, "The Court doesn't have the

jurisdiction or authority to grant your request," but indicated that Schmid's request might be considered by a higher court. Then, looking at the papers before him, he said, "This is a moment I'd rather not face. This is only the second time in twenty years on the bench that I've had to pronounce the death penalty. But it is my duty." After a pause, he then directed that Schmid be taken to the Arizona State Penitentiary in Florence and executed on the morning of June 17, 1966, by the administration of lethal gas.

Judge Garrett's secretary recalled that "He [Garrett] was so shaken by the dual pronouncements of death sentences, that I asked a newsman to go into his chambers and say hello. He needed someone to say something to him."

As soon as Schmid returned to his jail cell, he wrote:

The only part of today's events that caused any preponderant anxiety was the fact that my deliverance wasn't more eloquent. I had the usual pretrial trembles and in my opinion my elocution was below par, though I did enter my demand for pentothal. Originally I'd planned to include a manifold of statements, but the remembrance of Plato's 4 cardinal virtues of prudence, fortitude, temperance, and justice, overruled the decision. Plus the undue embarrassment of my erstwhile attorney caused me to withhold any further disclosure of evidence obtained.

On the last Sunday in March, Schmid spoke to a confidant through the greenish, steel-barred, bullet-proof window of the visiting room. He held the telephone hard against his ear and as he spoke he tapped on the thick glass with one finger for emphasis. "I want to take the stand under a sodium pentothal injection and challenge all their witnesses to do the same."

A nervous rash had reddened one side of his neck, and a long lock of the freshly black-dyed hair shadowed one eye. The gray T-shirt had a hole in the chest and his baggy blue dungarees stamped PIMA CO. JAIL sagged below his waist.

He had decided that he needed a new lawyer. "I've been seriously thinking of contacting another attorney —not one around here. The one I've had in mind is this Foreman; he appears to be very aggressive and that's what I need. Perhaps he might be interested if you told him about all the lawsuits providing I win."

Percy Foreman was widely known throughout the country for never losing a client. Contacted, Foreman said, "I've at least twenty-six other murder cases pending which the judges had to reset over the last eighteen months and as a result it is highly unlikely that I would be able to accept any additional cases. I don't think it would be fair to the courts to which I'm committed." He went on to say, "It would have been a most interesting case, but the boy has already been tried and convicted. I don't imagine he'll be tried on the other one until the others have been determined on appeal. . . . If it were a new case, if I had the maneuvering ability, the right to make the record, it's the type of case I would accept for whatever the boy would be able to pay."

Foreman said he didn't know the prosecutor in the case nor the Arizona laws but that he sometimes thought "the power of the news media have greater weight than the criminal code or code of criminal procedure. If you put it big enough in ink, why there are politicians, ambitious for advancement, who will continue to act. . . .

"I'm not a headline hunter and I've lots of rules about my practice. I'm not sure there are lawyers in Arizona who can render better service to Charlie Schmid than I can. I didn't read the testimony but it seemed a classic case for some psychiatrist with all the bizarre painting of the face and lips and the putting of tin cans in his boots." Foreman asked whether "competent psychiatrists" had testified, and was told that no psychiatric testimony had been submitted during the trial.

"It's not my policy as I said before to criticize lawyers but the lawyer ought to have to take half the juice, it was a classic case for a psychiatrist from all that bizarre testimony."

Schmid was transferred from Pima County Jail to the penitentiary 60 miles north at Florence. There, from his cell on Death Row, in a cluster of new green cells at half-basement level, he could view the death house less than one hundred feet away.

Separate from the other buildings, the "Little House"

was a small adobe building, with a slanted roof like a narrow garage and a metal smokestack reaching skyward. No doors on the north side of the building; just a worn brick wall. On the west end was a low door like an iron slab closely fitted into the wall, which was opened by a large flat-headed key. The floor of the witness room was concrete. A large display case extended along the brown wall, containing rows of photographs of those executed by hanging.

The actual rope noose used surrounded each individual photograph. Twenty-eight nooses nailed around twenty-eight photographs. On June 22, 1928, four Chinese were hanged between 5:16 and 6:33 that morning, one rope used for all four men.

One photograph was of a woman, Eva Dugan, framed by the rope used for her execution on February 11, 1930.

In 1933 Arizona changed from hanging to execution by gas. There were thirty-five more photographs in the display case, of those put to death in the gas chamber. Three soldiers were executed on July 8, 1943, and the last execution had occurred on March 14, 1963.

Opposite the display case, three narrow windows revealed the rear of an octagonal metal chamber, like a one-man sea-diving bell. In the center stood a perforated steel chair with thick worn leather straps attached through the back. More straps and buckles rested on the arms of the chair, and two hung down from the front legs. The chair faced an oval-shaped steel door. A narrow aluminum-painted pipe extended from the wall behind the chair, up through the ceiling of the chamber. Another pipe, old and rusted in places, extended from the right wall to empty over a concrete pit sunken into the floor beneath the chair.

On the south wall of the Little House were three doors: one to a closetlike preparation room, one opening onto the gas-chamber door, and another, at the east end of the building, shoulder-wide with an enameled metal sign CONDEMNED CELL in the type of block letters used on the washroom doors. Beyond the door in the center of the dim, gray room, were two smaller cells. Moss-colored stains encrusted the toilet bowl in each cell. The bars were a thatch of square steel rods, painted but peeling and rusted in places. The cell doors were thick metal slabs with slots punched through at eye level. The deathwatch room and condemned cells had not been cleaned since the previous execution. On the crossbar in one cell, above a striped dusty mattress, sat a sardine can stuffed with crushed-out cigarette butts.

In the room were an old card table, a cane chair with a dusty seat, an old boxy television set and some wrinkled and dogeared magazines. One wall was a wide sliding door, made of mismatched and dented parts of welded iron, with holes, cracks, and two-inch gaps at the hinges; the door through which the condemned was led from the waiting cell to the gas chamber. No sounds of the preparations escaped the condemned waiting for the door to open.

Five days after being admitted to Death Row, Charles Schmid wrote in his journal:

I sit on my bunk and look out the window and there is a little house out there and I know inside the little house may lay my fate. . . .

The reality of death had been obscured by hope, but the last hour before the final decree, it finally became a reality.

What would death be like? The last breath, the last light and color, the last movement and touch, the last flickering of consciousness, the last dream, the lost and fading face of love—and then nothing, the dreamless, unsleeping, unawakening night of death.

The image is so real—you try to tell yourself it doesn't matter, that death will be a fascinating experience, an adventure, a terminal point at the end of all our roads, but even that isn't sufficient to enable the rationalization. The envolvement of being born and dying, perhaps a similar chain that forms a perpetual circle. From nothing at birth into nothing at death. . . .

No more is death just a concept or idea or a conundrum. It is tapping you on the shoulder and whispering in your ear, and the vacant haunting eyes mock you, ever patient, ever waiting. All your life you stack the blocks carefully, precisely, only to have them kicked everywhere and taken from you.

The horrible feeling of knowing you'll die, that it is all prearranged, decays you. It's a feeling of dying before the execution, because you *are* dying, every day more and more. All plans and dreams, the living from day to day is gone, and you know it. You shut your eyes and hope when you awake it will be gone, but it is not. You look to the window and there it is. . . .

You had thought that life had meaning, a reason. Death takes it away, one cold clean sweep and it is gone. That one tangible thing, the reason for life, the one sensible thing that made it endurable, is gone.

Everything's a farce, a dirty cruel joke, a hoax. Dead. Dead. That's all, just dead.

◆

Through an intermediary, Schmid began to negotiate with Percy Foreman, at the same time drawing up a proposal for sodium pentothal to be introduced as evidence in court. Contesting the guilty verdict, he seemed obsessed with the idea that a pentothal test would clear him. Schmid submitted the proposal, in which he stated: "Should the action of Sodium Pentathol produce evidence contrary to the jury's verdict, a retrial must be declared immediately." But he also stated, "Any negative result to the test should in no way alter, change, or hamper the defendant's right for appeal, etc." In conclusion, Schmid said, "No device or drug yet know to man is proven 100 percent accurate in determining truth or error. Any state of mental illness, whether it be neurotic, psychotic, or psychopathic in nature, can produce results other than the truth. . . ."

But Schmid concluded by stating, "Sodium Pentathol could and should be admissible as real and tangible evidence."

Aware of the value of publicity, Schmid tried another tactic. Arrangements were made for him to conduct an exclusive interview with George Scott of Tucson's station KCUB. On April 14, 1966, the interview was taped on Death Row, and aired the following day.

During the interview Scott asked about Bruns's testimony during the trial. Schmid said, "That is a highly controversial subject, but there was definite proof that he did misquote and lie under oath, and there was nothing I could do about it, because I could not take the stand. It was my lawyer's advice that I shouldn't take the stand because it wasn't needed."

Scott asked about Schmid's proposal concerning sodium pentothal. "I have a letter pending right now," Schmid replied. "I have already sent it off. I have sent several out to the county attorney, and in the letter I have asked Mr. Schafer or Mr. Green to contact Mr. Fritz and Mrs. Rowe and anybody else he wants to, and to come up here directly—because he does have the power, I am sure he does—and give me sodium pentothal, and I would be more than willing to have Mr. Fritz administer the sodium pentothal." But Schmid said he had not received an answer from that letter yet.

Later in the interview he said, "I realize that the press has to keep the public informed of various events, but I believe they should take an objective stand, or an impartial stand, and I do not believe they did this in this case, and it did very much prejudice my trial, anything I would have had to say. When I was in the courtroom and before they picked the jurors, I overheard some of the comments like 'I hope they pick me because I'd be more than happy to give him the pill,' I mean it was things like that that made me feel, well, I don't have a chance no matter what I said, I really wouldn't. And then when we asked for a change of venue and denied, how could I expect to have a trial? They should at least have given me that much of the benefit of a doubt. But it was denied me."

George Scott said, "Charles, many of us in the news media would glance over at you during the trial and wonder what feelings were going through you at the time, what feelings you were experiencing. Would you care to comment on that at this moment?"

"Well," Schmid replied, "to be perfectly honest with you, when I first went into trial, even though I did hear the comments by the prospective jurors, I really felt that I was going to get some kind of trial, or at least be able to present my case and prove that I didn't kill Gretchen or Wendy, and that Richard did, but as soon as the judge ruled that I wouldn't be able to admit any evidence against Richie in our trial it just—it just deflated me completely. . . ."

"Did you get a chance to see *Life* magazine?" Scott asked.

Schmid laughed, "Oh did I ever! I couldn't believe it, I really couldn't. I read the magazine and I looked at the pictures and in all honesty I thought they were talking about somebody else. I said, 'This couldn't be me, really it couldn't be. How could anybody be like that, really?' And then I read it from an objective view, and I thought, if I was reading it, and I was somebody else I would think the guy was guilty, and a rotten guy, and a monster too. I really couldn't belive it."

"Charles, you have been in Death Row for now approximately three weeks. What are your feelings now that you do have this much time on your hands?"

"The guards and other inmates have been pretty nice to me and let me see all the magazines and all the pretrial publicity that was denied me before this time, and I can get somewhat of an idea of what really happened, and what they said, and try and figure out a reason why they did it, although I really haven't found it. I read a little bit, like *Time* magazine that came out before the trial, then I glance up and look out the window and I see the gas chamber out there and the Little House, and it really makes me wonder and sometimes I just pray to anything or anybody, or anything I can, and ask why does it have to happen to me. . . ."

"Charles, you have been portrayed as wearing makeup, and also dyeing your hair."

". . . irregardless of whether I do or don't, I would like to know what difference does it make if I did or didn't do such things as they claim I did, considering makeup, etcetera? I really thought this was America, and if I felt like doing something like that, I could. If I wanted to dye my hair green, what difference would it make? But no, the newspapers and magazines, they have to say it was really a terrible crime that this perverted little animal wore makeup and dyed his hair. Everything I read—it seems like it is a crime to be short, you know. They say, 'Well, this short, little teen-age Lothario!' And Lothario, of course, is some man portrayed in somebody's play—I don't know what it was— but he was very unscrupulous, and a sex maniac, and things like that. They incorrectly called me 'a teen-age Lothario.' Well, I would like to say, where is the evidence to prove all of this, their obvious contentions that I do this and do that. . . ."

"Almost all the press media, Charles, portrayed you as wearing cowboy boots with rags or tin cans stuffed in the shoes."

". . . it was just to add to their fictional character of the monster that they made up. It helped the image so why shouldn't they put it in?"

Scott asked about Schmid's guitar playing, and if he ever performed professionally.

"Yes, I have," Schmid replied, "on several occasions I have played for different bands, and I have had my own band. That is just something that I really enjoy, that's all. The one thing that I really can't understand, it really amazes me no end, is that by the law in our land in America and democracy, a person is completely innocent until proven guilty, but yet everything that was said about me, prior to my trial, was guilty, guilty, guilty, guilty. There was nothing else involved but guilt. . . ."

"How did you feel the very first day of court?" Scott asked.

"At that time I wasn't aware of the pretrial publicity or anything that had happened, and I felt very confident that I would go in there, and I would present my case as it actually happened and I'd be perfectly able to convince everybody that I was completely innocent, and had nothing to do with it. So I sat down and the judge started to read the charges against me, and then instead of saying 'The defendant pleads not guilty,' he said, 'The defendant pleads guilty.' And I felt like somebody had dropped a bomb on me, and I couldn't believe it, and I said, 'Huh? What's happening, what's wrong?' and he said, 'Oh, excuse me, I mean the defendant pleads not guilty,' and then everybody kind of chuckled like that, and I said 'What's wrong, I mean, this doesn't sound quite right?' Of course, you know, it probably doesn't mean anything, but it was just—it was just—gave me a brief example of what was yet to come, and it made me aware of what to expect. And then as it progressed and further and further, I saw he wasn't going to allow my case to be presented, and so anything I obviously had to say wouldn't do any good."

"Charles, as you sit here day after day in Death Row, what feelings do you have?"

". . . the things that really bother me most is that I am going to be literally murdered for something I didn't do, and sooner or later there is going to be another crime committed, and it is going to be proven

without any doubt whatsoever that I am completely
innocent, and then it is going to be too late and everybody is going to say, 'Gee, we are really sorry, Smitty,
but it's to late now because you are dead, but here is
a dollar for your wife, or two dollars, but we are really
sorry we made a mistake, but that is just the way life
is.' And it's hard for me to believe that life or people
would be so cruel."

A few days after the interview was broadcast, Percy
Foreman decided against entering the Schmid case,
saying, "I just can't leave these other people in the
lurch. . . . But I've thought it over and I believe the
best contribution I could make to the boy there would
be to get him a lawyer that could make the most of
the situation. Do you know Lee Bailey?"

At the time, F. Lee Bailey of Boston was awaiting
the Supreme Court's decision on the appeal for Dr.
Sam Sheppard. Foreman said, "This whole Schmid
case sounds like the sort of case Bailey could really
get himself into. He's a young man, probably the second
best attorney in the country, very aggressive."

Bailey was contacted and expressed interest in the
case. He had heard of Arizona lawyers showing a
willingness to accept a case at the onset of a trial, but
losing their commitment in the courtroom. Bailey said,
"They're local lawyers and they can't afford to stick
their necks out. That's why there's renegade lawyers
like me. You can't blame local attorneys, especially
when there's gruesome murders involved." He said
he would be in Tucson in two days. When he arrived,

Bailey was shown the bulging file of pretrial publicity in the Schmid case. Scanning through the material while en route to the prison, Bailey said, "This is what you need to crack a case like this apart. There's just about as much here as Sam Sheppard's."

At the prison, waiting for Schmid to be brought from Death Row, Bailey stared at the walls and gun turrets, the corroded spikes of the high iron gates, and a large rectangular mirror above the gate, which a prison guard was watching. Finally, Schmid was brought to the gate before the visiting room. The cuffs on the sleeves of his old army jacket were folded back several times. "He's very small, isn't he," Bailey said. Then, inside the visiting room moments later, he said to Schmid, "Looks like you've got yourself a lot of trouble."

Schmid grinned. "I guess I have, sir." He then insisted on his innocence to the Boston lawyer, saying that all he wanted was a fair trial. He told of his efforts to obtain an examination under sodium pentothal. Bailey recommended instead a lie-detector test which he said was "infallible, if administered the right way by a qualified expert."

Schmid seemed uncertain. "If something went wrong, mechanically, say that the county attorney could find something there to use against me, I mean it's what they've done with every single thing."

"The test I'd have administered would be a sure bet," Bailey said, "and the best thing to throw right back at a conviction like this Fritz trial. By that I don't mean it would necessarily change anything, but it would be putting your best foot forward. I'd bring the most qualified man in to give you the test, and if everything you've said is true, the results of the test would be the first direct move." He said there would have to be a retrial, but he couldn't see how it could be brought to court in Arizona.

Bailey asked Schmid about funds needed to finance another trial and appeals. Schmid's answers didn't impress him. After an hour and a half Bailey was returned to Tucson, where he discussed the case first with Schmid's parents and later at dinner with Tinney. Bailey inquired as to why Schmid had not testified in his own defense and Tinney told him that he had been trying to protect the trial record for the appeal. If Schmid had taken the stand, Schafer might have antagonized him and then Schmid might have incriminated himself beyond repair.

Bailey also mentioned the lack of psychiatric testimony in the case that seemed to call for it. Tinney told Bailey that "there had been psychiatric examinations, and the results would scare the pants off any lawyer."

Before leaving town the following morning, Bailey was interviewed and said he didn't see any necessity for becoming involved in Schmid's defense, adding, "He has perfectly competent counsel in Mr. Tinney, whom I hold in great respect." He also said, "This case involves pretrial publicity and so of course I was interested in it. . . . The decision of the Supreme Court in the Sheppard case will be very important to defend-

ants in future sensational cases. . . . The Charlie
Schmid case is a bad case of trial by newspaper. If
the Sheppard decision comes down right, you can
forget about the Schmid conviction."

Two weeks later, Bailey wrote to those who acted
for Schmid in bringing him to Tucson. He said that
he believed Schmid's parents were committed to Tinney
and that arranging a defense would necessarily involve
"some coordinated thought between Charlie and his
folks." But he went on say that: "Although I am satis-
fied that Bill Tinney is very able, I am sure that he has
no desire to defend a man who questions his ability.
I will be happy to defend Charlie if that is his wish.
However, I would be reluctant to do so unless Bill is
retained as co-counsel because as a result of our conference I am impressed with his understanding of the
case."

Bailey stated that while he would like to defend
Schmid on a cost-free basis, he was unable to do so,
and requested some formal fee arrangement. Attempts
were made to set up a defense fund, but with a not-
able lack of success. After three weeks, it had accumulated a total of $36, and no one would volunteer to hold
the fund in trust.

In the meantime, Schmid's wife, Diane, and her
mother announced at a news conference that she was
suing for divorce. "We'll get his car and she should
have that house, too," Diane's mother said. "He owes
her that much."

Diane was asked if she still loved her husband, but

her mother cut her reply short, saying, "That doesn't matter. *His* mother's trying to break them up. She wants to keep Diane over there away from her own family. When we went over to get her clothes she wouldn't even let Diane have the wedding pictures just because Smitty hadn't seen them. I'll get even with her for the way she talked to me."

That evening, in a televised interview, mother and daughter stated that the grounds for divorce would be mental cruelty—because of Schmid's "anger, his uncontrollable temper and because he's capable of violence and probably guilty of the charges against him."

When Schmid got the news he said, "It was like a blow in the stomach. I just couldn't believe it. When I saw her the week before she told me everything had been straightened out and she was going to live with my mother who would take care of her. I've been afraid for her and I thought she'd be safer living with my family. I know she's young and I know it's hard for her, but I didn't expect she'd do this."

He speculated that "some movie people came to town and offered Diane a contract if she would divorce me so that it would agree with a fictionalized version of a movie being made on the story in *Life* Magazine." Sighing, Schmid continued, "I've hit the very bottom now and there's only one way left and that's up."

Schmid continued to hope that F. Lee Bailey would represent him at the second trial set for October 4th. Bailey had said, "It is difficult for me to believe that Arizona will actually bring Charlie to trial for the

Rowe murder in October. It would be obviously impossible to assemble two, let alone twelve, citizens who are ignorant of the fact that Schmid was judged guilty of a double murder earlier this year."

Then on June 20 Bailey wrote, saying that he was accepting the retainer and was entering the case. Shortly thereafter, on July 6, the U.S. Supreme Court ruled, in an 8-1 decision, that Samuel Sheppard had not received a fair trial because of the "massive, pervasive, and prejudicial publicity that attended his prosecution."

Bailey brought his own polygraph expert in from Florida, stating, "I'm sending for the only man I trust to give Charlie the lie-detector test he has asked for. If he's lied to me, I'll just turn the results over to his mother and forget it."

On Thursday night, August 11, after seeing the results of ten hours of exhaustive tests with Schmid, Bailey announced publicly and with confidence that he would take the case of Charles Schmid.

Schmid said, "Mr. Bailey told me, 'Charlie, I don't know whether you'll be out of here next summer or eleven years from now, but you'll be out.'"

Part 6

"AN ARTICLE A DAY keeps justice away," Tinney told Judge Garrett on September 16 at a continuance hearing for Schmid. "The newspapers keep hitting over and over again on Schmid. I don't see how a jury can be impaneled now. We're having a contest between the court and the press. The Tucson press has put on a spirited campaign to cover anything in order to bring in the name of Charles Schmid. I complain of this because he has another trial awaiting him." Tinney asserted that the "daily doses of Schmid" would affect even the judges. "All but two Superior Court judges are seeking reelection. In such a campaign by a judge, no matter how honorable he is, he can't help but be swayed by public opinion. And the opinion of this community is adverse to my client."

Tinney argued for more than an hour, and then Judge Garrett denied his motions. The Rowe trial remained set for October 4th.

Five days later Tinney and Bailey filed a petition asking the U.S. District Court to take over jurisdiction of the case and have it removed out of the state of Arizona. They argued that with all the pretrial publicity, Schmid could not be assured his constitutional rights. After some legal maneuvers, the U.S. Circuit Court agreed to hear arguments on the petition, and meanwhile postponed the Rowe trial.

On Death Row, Schmid continued to write.

Nights are no different than days. Sleep is a friend sometimes but one I cannot trust completely. I sense it as a tempting seductress I welcome when my limbs grow partially paralytic. There is a semidarkness now within my cell. The heat is unbearable but I know the pleasures of sleep will overcome me shortly. The only pleasure outside of sexual fantasies that remains is the fantasies of my dream world when I lapse into an unconsciousness from sleep.

The dreams are so similiar to actual reality, I'm unable to distinguish any particular difference. Perhaps my dreams are actually reality and what I assume to be real, my supposedly conscious hours, is merely a horrible nightmare. It's strange but I can only recall three dreams where I've distinguished colors. The depths were accented with an irrevocable beauty. Each day now as I try to rember the sequences, the clarity becomes sharper and more focused. . . .

If death is simply a continuance of this dream-world, it would be rather pleasant and I would find it acceptable. I would very much enjoy sleeping twenty-four hours a day provided the dreams were included. Perhaps they are real, perhaps it is an escape. I simply cannot comprehend.

He was allowed his guitar and amplifier in his cell but had to decline an invitation to join the prison band. Time was passing. The District Court postponement of the Rowe trial had "suspended it in limbo," Schmid wrote.

He had enrolled in some correspondence courses on business and economics, and his parents sent him textbooks and a daily copy of the *Wall Street Journal*. He was permitted to spend one hour a day outside.

The Federal court ruled against Tinney and Bailey's request for a change of venue and Schmid's trial was set for April 3. But Bailey, at this time, would be in Sarasota, Florida, defending Dr. Carl Coppolino. Tinney claimed that he himself was unprepared to defend Schmid without Bailey, and sought a further postponement of the trial. While Schmid was being brought from State prison, news was released that four subpoenas had been issued by Schmid's attorneys, calling on Schafer, County Attorney Norman Green, and the attorneys for Saunders and Mary French to testify to "deals made."

As soon as Schmid arrived at Pima County Jail, he granted another interview to George Scott of station KCUB, whose first question was about Schmid's continuance hearing.

Schmid said, "I believe the whole purpose of Mr. Schafer's rebuttal in court concerning my continuance is for actually one reason only, and that's because he's really afraid to face Mr. Bailey in the courtroom—because Mr. Baily has a reputation for uncovering fraud and discovering truth. Personally I believe that the newspapers and a lot of other people have been unfair to Mr. Tinney. He has received no money whatsoever from the taxpayers or anyone else as reimbursement for acting as co-counsel for Mr. Bailey. As far as his integrity goes, let me tell you this much: if we were refused a continuance . . . in order that Mr. Bailey would be able to be present, Mr. Tinney would have laid his license on the line and we would have refused to put up a defense at all and just sat there in court . . .

"It seems justice is a very expensive thing when you're on the side of the fence where poor people live, and I'm on that side now. If I hadn't been fortunate enough to have Mr. Bailey, I'd be a lot more frightened though. I can't help but wonder what would happen if a person was in a similiar situation that I was, and wasn't fortunate enough to have Mr. Bailey and his team of investigators to investigate and uncover the truth, as Mr. Schafer has his police force, policewomen, and his team of investigators to do what they want twenty-four hours a day."

Schmid then told Scott: "When Mr. Bailey and one of the most qualified polygraph experts administered me a polygraph examination, they telephoned Mr. Schafer and asked him to be present before they gave me any knowledge I was to have a test, and he flatly refused. And he also flatly refused to accept the results of that test."

"How do you expect to come out?" Scott asked.

"I can only guarantee you one thing, and one thing only, and that's that I'll never give up, not now, not ever, no matter what. Not until the truth is firmly established once and for all. And sooner or later it's going to be, I know this."

At the hearing before Judge Roylston, Tinney stated that he himself had not been in recent contact with the defendant, that Bailey had conferred with Schmid, starting with an interview in July.

In protesting Tinney's motion for continuance, Schafer said that Tinney's statement that he had not communicated with his client since last July was "shocking."

Tinney said that Bailey "has had his private investigators in Tucson," and added that recent defense efforts had been conducted "all to the exclusion generally of myself. Our position," Tinney told the judge, "is that the defendant has contracted with Bailey to appear and defend him in his trial. . . . The taxpayers aren't paying a penny for the attorneys who are defending Mr. Schmid."

Schafer asserted that the prosecution was not aware of any extensive efforts to have the Coppolino trial postponed, and charged that Tinney had told him last October, "You won't get Charlie to trial for two years."

Despite further protests by the county attorney, Judge Roylston granted a continuance and reset the trial date for May 10, 1967.

The sensational nature of the case and the addition of F. Lee Bailey to the cast of characters assured massive coverage by the news media. Judge Roylston therefore established an extensive set of regulations to try to prevent Schmid's case being prejudiced before the trial had even begun.

Bailey lost his defense of Dr. Coppolino and flew to Tucson on May 9 in his private eight-seater Lear jet. The white aircraft touched down at 7:03 that evening, and moments later Bailey climbed down to face the group of reporters. One newsman asked, "You going to be set to go tomorrow?"

"Oh, yes," Bailey said confidently, "Oh, yes." Overlooked by the reporters, Tinney, who had arrived to meet Bailey, walked quietly around the Lear jet, examining the plane admiringly.

"Do you think losing the Coppolino case will have any effect on this trial?" Bailey was asked.

"I hope not. It shouldn't," he replied.

"How many times have you seen Charles Schmid?"

"Oh, I'd say four or five times, I haven't kept count."

"Where do you draw the line in fighting for a client?"

Bailey said, "Oh, it's a very clear line. We don't suborn any perjury, manufacture any evidence, or represent something to a jury which we know is not true."

The newsman asked: "Would you go on representing a client who pleaded innocent to a crime even though you knew he was guilty of the crime?"

"I might," Bailey said after a moment. "I might if he insisted on it."

"If you win this case with Charles Schmid," the newsman asked, "will you be working on the Fritz appeal?"

"I'm not going to discuss this case until a jury is impaneled and locked up." Bailey left the airport in Tinney's air-conditioned Volkswagen.

On the morning of May 10, the Tucson *American* reported:

> One of the strangest trials in the history of U.S. jurisprudence will open today when Boston trial lawyer F. Lee Bailey begins the defense of Charles Schmid for a murder already used by the state to convict and sentence him to death for two other murders. . . .

The second trial was taking place in Division 7 of Superior Court, containing only thirty seats, and attendance was limited to the defense and prosecution staff, Schmid's parents, and a selected number of newsmen.

Questioning prospective jury members, Bailey emphasized what he termed a "holocaust of pretrial publicity," and objected to the prosecution's excluding jurors opposed to the death penalty. He made it clear that he would base Schmid's defense on the absence of a corpus delecti, and repeatedly asked whether the juror would be prejudiced against Schmid if he didn't testify in his own behalf. Bailey also challenged jurors displaying knowledge of Schmid's previous conviction.

Judge Roylston called a panel of 125 jurors, considerably more than is usual in a murder trial. From these a panel of 41 would be chosen, of which the prosecution and defense would each be allowed to challenge 13 without cause. The remaining 15 would make up the 12-member jury, with 3 alternates.

"Do you think Charlie Schmid is innocent until proven guilty?" Bailey asked one prospective juror.

"Yes, sir."

"Do you think he might be innocent even though I'm here to defend him?"

"Oh, yes, sir."

To another juror he asked bluntly: "To put it simply, do you believe he did it?"

The jurors were not sure, and both were challenged for cause.

Bailey did everything he could to disqualify jurors. He seemed to think that if a panel could not be chosen from the original 125 he would have made his point about undue pretrial publicity and a mistrial might be declared. Judge Roylston gave Bailey some hope when he said that if a panel was not chosen from the first 125, any additional jurors summoned might have read or heard reports of the proceedings and thus be eligible to challenge.

After emphasizing the absence of the body, Bailey's questions would stress that the state had to prove that a murder occurred in the county before it could begin to prove that Schmid committed it.

Yet if the remaining evidence was strong enough, Schafer would ask, would the absence of the corpse keep the jurors from returning a guilty verdict?

"We don't use probabilities," Bailey told a woman juror, "so long as there is a *possibility* that the alleged victim might turn up somewhere, would you be inclined to vote for the death penalty—or hold up?"

At noon recess, Katharine Schmid told a friend: "I don't know why Mr. Bailey keeps avoiding me. We've tried for two days to speak to him, but every time we get close to him he just keeps his face straight ahead and just brushes past us as though he doesn't even know who we are. I don't understand that. . . . Charlie said that Mr. Bailey hasn't talked to *him* at all, and he's wondering what's going on."

The following day, Bailey asked the court to forbid the jury to sentence Schmid to death if he was convicted. "We will maintain that the power to execute should be withheld," Bailey said, "since there is no body and because death is an irrevocable sentence if she should turn up." He indicated sternly that defense would appeal any conviction, and that Schmid was indigent. "We're just making a record here in this case," he said.

The selection of the panel moved slowly. The tape recorder and court stenographer's machine silently recorded the words and technicalities, questions, answers, objections, instructions, recesses. The procedure was numbing. Schmid sat impassively with his arms folded, alongside Tinney, who said nothing throughout. At the end of the day, a reporter said in the corridor, "No jury's going to be selected, not in this trial."

Before court reconvened on the fifth day of jury selection, according to an informed source, Tinney and Bailey saw Schafer alone in Judge Roylston's chambers and Tinney said with a grin: "How about second [degree]? Have you given that any thought? It would save the state the expense of a long trial and appeal and retrial . . . and it would knock down one of our grounds for appeal in the Fritz [case]." Schafer replied in the negative, and Bailey laughed and commented, "You know what Charlie would say to pleading guilty, don't you . . . ?" and Bailey thrust up the middle finger of one hand.

When Judge Roylston was seated in the courtroom and the session began, Bailey moved for another mistrial, charging that the Arizona *Star* was "making a deliberate effort to keep the defendant from getting a fair trial." He accused the paper of publicizing information which Roylston had asked reporters not to mention on three occasions. "If this keeps up," Bailey said, "The defense might as well throw in the towel."

During the long six days, Judge Roylston, the prosecutor, and Bailey had individually examined 130 jurors, 97 had been excused, and Bailey had objected to the calling of a new group. The judge still had under advisement Bailey's mistrial motion, based on the ground that the *Star* had repeatedly printed prejudicial information. On its own part, the *Star* was convinced that Bailey's only motive for appearing in Arizona was to muster personal publicity. The newspaper decided not to print the lawyer's name and referred to him as "one of Schmid's attorneys."

On Thursday, May 18, the jury selection began for the first time without some sort of motion from Bailey. He sat quietly most of the morning, questioning only two prospective jurors. Many had been disqualified before Bailey had interviewed them. Only 35 panel members had been chosen and the outlook for a jury was dim until Judge Roylston discovered that Arizona law required only 32 members, so the original juror panel was reduced to 35 with one alternate instead of three. Under these rules the panel was completed.

The judge told the nine men and three women that he would allow them to return home that night, but that they would be sequestered the next morning at which time the testimony would begin. Court was adjourned until 10 A.M. Friday.

That Thursday evening, in answer to an urgent request, Charles Schmid, Sr., climbed into Smitty's dusty Falcon and drove to County Jail. He entered the visitor's aisle and nodded to his son on the other side of the bulletproof glass. Then he picked up the telephone.

"I'm preparing a writ to dismiss both Mr. Bailey and Bill," Smitty said. "I'll defend myself in this trial."

"You can't fire them!" Mr. Schmid said and asked for an explanation.

"The county attorney's offered a deal and Mr. Bailey told me he's taking it, he wants me to plead guilty to second-degree murder." Schmid spoke rapidly: the jury was impossible, and Bailey had informed him before the afternoon session that Schafer had proposed that Schmid plead to reduced charges. "Mr. Bailey told me it was the only way to save my life, he said if he went ahead I'd be convicted and sentenced to death." Schmid went on to explain that Bailey had informed him that Schafer was bringing in the Fritz case, even though it was after the fact, and having it admitted as suppression of evidence. "They're going to use it the same way they used this one in the last trial, just the other way around. Bailey said it'll destroy the appeal on the Fritz case and I'd be dead within ninety days."

Charles, Sr., didn't understand. "If the county attorney's so damn sure they'll get the death sentence, then why's he offering deals?"

"To save the state the cost of the trial and appeals, and Mr. Bailey's made it clear we'll appeal. He told me the jury's completely prejudiced and dying to give me the gas." Schmid told his father that he had been "caught off guard" by his lawyer's information and that he had said "Hell no! We'll win! No deal, there's no body!" Then, Schmid told his father, Tinney had said "You haven't a prayer and because of the Fritz stuff being admitted you'll be dead in ninety days."

Schmid's father advised him to "hold off on the writ business until we can get this settled with Bill."

At 9:15 that night, Katharine Schmid contacted Tinney. He told her it was true, Schafer had proposed the deal. According to Mrs. Schmid, Tinney told her, "But we're not accepting it. Whenever a prosecutor makes a deal we have to present it to the defendant, so I told him [Charlie] today. But we're not taking it. . . ."

Friday morning, before the trial began, Judge Roylston ruled that he would allow testimony on the Fritz murders to be admitted as evidence. Bailey sought a last-ditch motion asking for a mistrial, change of venue and continuance on the ground that members of the jury knew of Schmid's prior convictions. He said, "The defendant is already two strikes down," and indicated that because of this the jury perhaps would be "more willing to convict him" for the alleged Rowe murder.

A fair trial in some other city in Arizona might be possible, Bailey said, but the trial should be moved out of the state. He criticized the makeup of the jury also; persons well-informed of the convictions of Saunders and French should be disqualified from service. His final attempt to halt the trial was to question Judge Roylston's jurisdiction over the case; unless Schmid's conviction for the Fritz killings was reversed by an appellate court, he would be executed, and Bailey questioned whether the judge could "try a carcass for the crime."

Bailey's motions were denied and the prosecution began its opening statements. In August of 1965, Schafer told the jury, Charles Schmid murdered Gretchen Fritz because he had told her of the Rowe murder, and she was holding it over his head. . . .

"The defendant wanted to kill a girl in 1964 to see if he could do it and see how it felt. He asked Mary French to get him a girl." Schmid gave her a list of prospective victims and Alleen Rowe was one of them.

Schafer then briefly told of the murder of Alleen Rowe as described by Mary French and said that Schmid had confessed the murder to two friends, and later to Gretchen Fritz. He described Schmid's relationship to Gretchen and told of that murder. Schafer concluded that Mary French's testimony and other evidence would prove that Schmid was guilty of "premeditated murder" and should receive the death sentence.

Bailey declined to make an opening statement, and then Schafer called Norma Rowe as the first witness for the state. Mrs. Rowe burst into tears when the prosecutor showed her a picture of Alleen. When asked about her daughter's relationship with the three who allegedly killed her, Mrs. Rowe said that on one occasion Alleen told her, "Some people you go along with. You don't cross them. They could run you down with a car."

Norma Rowe was followed on the stand by Mary

French who repeated much of the testimony offered in the Fritz trial, with a few additional details. She now said that Saunders first hit Alleen with a rock and she started running, but Schmid caught up with her and struck the fatal blow with a stone.

Bailey tried to discredit Mary, implying that she hated Alleen Rowe and was lying about Schmid's part in the crime because he refused to marry her when she was pregnant with his child.

Bailey asked, "Did you hate Alleen Rowe?"

"No."

"Did you go to her assistance?"

"No."

Bailey asked Mary why she had gone to such lengths to lure Alleen from the house.

Mary replied, "I didn't really believe they would do it." She sighed listlessly.

Schafer had intended calling John Saunders as his third witness, but Saunders had changed his mind about a lot of things: He now contended he was railroaded by his previous attorneys into making his guilty plea, and his present counsel informed Schafer that Saunders would take the Fifth Amendment if summoned.

Roylston announced that unless the defense could produce law to the contrary, Saunders' sealed preliminary hearing transcript could be admitted and read to the jury. Bailey asked for time to study the legality of the matter, since he and Tinney had not considered the possibility of such a move by Schafer.

"Mr. Bailey," Judge Roylston said, "we have about a fifteen minute recess coming up. If you can find any cases on this matter in that time, I'll be happy to look at them."

"Your Honor," Bailey countered, "my law professors would shudder to think that such an important point would be allotted only fifteen minutes for research."

"Mr. Bailey," the judge replied, "that's why you had law professors, to teach you how to look up things you needed in a hurry."

The day ended with attorneys arguing about whether Saunders' transcript could be admitted. As the jury was being kept sequestered, Judge Roylston scheduled a court session for the next day, Saturday.

But at 9:15 the following morning, no one was in court but the newsmen and Schmid's parents. As minutes ticked by, everyone began to surmise that something was up. Schmid's parents finally reached Tinney in the hallway who told them Bailey was "sick," that he wouldn't be coming to court today. More to the point, he told them that they had decided to accept Schafer's deal—"Charlie will escape the gas chamber," Mrs. Schmid was told—and that Mr. Bailey was having it arranged for Charlie to be placed in a mental institution.

"I want to talk to Charlie," Katharine said, "and you better get Mr. Bailey here."

"He's sick today. . . ."

Mr. and Mrs. Schmid were allowed to consult with Charlie in a jury room not in use. They report their son saying, "I don't want any part of this! I said I'm *not* accepting it and I'm not pleading guilty."

Tinney disappeared temporarily while Katharine listened to her husband protest the county attorney's proposal. Minutes later, Tinney again entered the jury room, accompanied by Bailey.

"He looked in the pink of health," Katharine recalls. "And the only reason he went and got Mr. Bailey was to force the issue about changing Charlie's mind."

Bailey insisted: "This jury was set to hang him even before we started this trial," and that the only realistic choice facing Schmid was death in the gas chamber or life in prison. Schmid seemed uncertain.

"What should I do, Mom?" he asked.

Katharine Schmid was bewildered. "I can't answer that for you, I just can't, Charlie. You'll have to make that decision. . . ."

Tinney confirmed Bailey's gloomy prognosis of their chances in court. Finally, when Schmid appeared to understand that the Fritz appeal was at stake, he seemed to weaken, and at that moment Bailey informed the family it was time to enter the courtroom. Schmid muttered a barely audible, "OK."

After a brief meeting in the judge's chambers, the court convened at 11:30. Bailey arose and stated that Schmid would enter a plea of guilty to second-degree murder. The defendant, he said, had made a "certain admission" to him the previous summer during the lie detector test. "The defendant is in dire need of psychiatric help, although under the law as it now stands, he is not legally insane," Bailey said. "When it became apparent that the state's evidence was overwhelming, counsel advised the defendant to plead guilty to a non-capital charge. . . . The defendant is guilty of the crime and believes it is in his best interest to so plead."

Tinney concurred with Bailey's statements and Judge Roylston asked Schafer if he would consent to a guilty plea to the reduced charge. Schafer answered with a quiet "Yes." The judge then asked Schmid to rise.

"Do you desire to enter this plea?" Roylston asked.

After a brief pause, Schmid said, "Yes."

"Have any promises been made to you?"

Schmid shook his head. "None."

"Have any threats been made to you?"

"None."

"Is this a voluntary plea?"

"Yes."

"Are you pleading because you are guilty or for some other reason?"

Schmid stared at the floor, then looked up at the bench. "Because I am guilty," he said.

The judge tentatively set the date for sentencing for June 2, 1967. But Bailey asked that Schmid be given psychiatric examinations. "My position," Bailey said, "is that the defendant is in need of such help."

Tinney also asked for "a few days to contemplate the issue and talk with the experts whom we plan to consult."

The jurors were excused. Court was adjourned, Schmid was handcuffed and led from the courtroom.

Immediately following the session, Bailey gave an interview at the Tucson Press Club, one block from the courthouse. Tinney was as his side but remained silent. When asked what effect Schmid's plea would have on his career, Bailey replied, "What the hell has this got to do with my career? I can't see where this has anything to do with my win-loss record. It just doesn't apply. An attorney's first concern is adequately defending his client, you fellows can't see beyond a win-loss record to the defense of a client. . . . Justice means guilty people should plead or be convicted and the innocent should be acquitted. That's what we've done in this case. My career has nothing to do with it."

He suspected that Schmid was guilty, Bailey said, despite a lie-detector test that Bailey had administered which showed Schmid was telling the truth when he said he was innocent (contradicting what he had said in court).

Bailey was asked whether they had difficulty in convincing Schmid to plead guilty.

"I wouldn't say we had to argue with him," Bailey said with a smile. "Pleading guilty was not a decision of mine to make. He had to decide." As the trial date approached, Bailey said, he became more convinced that Schmid was guilty. "Yes," he said confidently, "I knew he was guilty before the trial started. I let the state present its evidence to show the defendant what he was up against." He told the newsmen he first mentioned a change in plea Friday at the close of court. "I just mentioned it in passing. This morning I put it to him as a serious proposal. He took it without an argument. . . . He had been giving it a lot of thought," Bailey continued. "We had to let him see the state's evidence before he would decide, though. As long as he could sit in his cell and think that counsel could magically make the witnesses go away, he was reluctant to plead. I wouldn't say we had to argue with him, though."

"Mr. Bailey," a reporter asked, "most if not all the facts printed about the case were eventually admitted in the trials, surely Schmid was well aware of the state's evidence long before this—before your arrival here in Tucson?"

Bailey shrugged. He stressed that he had received no pay for his services, and had found the trial "financially disastrous, but pleasant in most other respects."

Bailey said Schmid was sick, and needed psychiatric help, adding that anyone who committed an irrational crime was mentally unsound.

"Miss French's testimony would have been corroborated, and furthermore, I felt that the jury was behind her," Bailey said. "What I'm worried about now is the corrosive effect this might have on him in regard to the Fritz case."

Several hours later at the Tucson airport, Bailey gave a last-minute interview with a reporter before he took off in his Lear jet. He said he knew Schmid was guilty about the third time he talked to him, and that it was Schmid's decision to plead guilty, "based on the advice of his counsel under the circumstances of the case at the moment."

The reporter asked, "How did you get a second-degree from Schafer?"

"Oh, I think he felt it was the wisest course in the best interest of the county. If I'd been the prosecutor I would certainly agree. The trial was costing a lot of money, the appeal, it would cost several hundred thousand dollars and probably would have gone to another retrial."

"Do you consider this case a loss?"

"A guilty man pleads guilty, he can't be considered a loss to anyone." Then, minutes later, F. Lee Bailey flew away.

"The first time they offered me the deal," County Attorney Schafer said to a friend, "I turned it down because I wasn't sure what they were up to." Then, he said, two days later on the last day of jury selection, Tinney again mentioned Schmid pleading guilty. Schafer had said, "Yeah, OK," but nothing came of it until Saturday. "The reason I accepted their deal," Schafer said, "was because I really doubted that the jury would vote for the death penalty when there wasn't a body." Second-degree meant keeping Schmid in prison that much longer. "And just to hear him say it in a public arena was worth it. But I just can't figure out how in the world they got him to plead guilty."

Schafer said that Mary French was still in love with

Schmid and he, Schafer was never sure if she'd testify, right up to the moment when she was seated on the witness stand. But the most important reason for accepting the deal, Schafer said, was, "If the Fritz case conviction is reversed and we have to retry it, we couldn't have referred to the Rowe murder." One of the points on Schmid's appeal was that the evidence concerning the Rowe case was wrongly introduced as evidence in the Fritz case. "The defense argued at the Fritz trial that the Rowe case should not have been admitted because Schmid hadn't been tried and he hadn't been convicted of it. Without Schmid's guilt being established in the Rowe matter, there would be very little if any evidence in a Fritz case retrial because there would be no motive."

No sooner had Schmid returned to County Jail on Saturday than he seized upon a new strategy which he would confide only to Sheriff Burr. He started talking about a "sellout" by Tinney and Bailey. He trusted no one, not even his parents, because "They went along with Tinney and Bailey's sellout."

Dan Sakall, the adult probation officer assigned to Schmid's presentencing report, listened to Schmid along with the sheriff, who had "little use for Bailey." Sheriff Burr thought the lawyer was "looking for an easy way out when he saw his shiny armor getting dented."

For several days the sheriff talked with Schmid. He said candidly that Schmid had told him "the whole story," except where Alleen Rowe was buried.

"Schmid's story makes some sense," Sheriff Burr said, "he's got some facts on his side. He's real friendly and talkative, except when the talk gets around to the body. He clams up, gives a blank look, or says, 'I'd like to help but I don't know.' "

Schafer said he was not sure if Schmid even knew where the body was. He said he would ask Tinney for Schmid's cooperation in finding the remains. "Bailey said to me on Saturday that he thinks Schmid knows where the body is, but wasn't sure."

Tinney replied that he didn't know if Schmid "knows where it is. However, I will do anything that is reasonable."

On Saturday, Tinney spent a few minutes with Schmid at the jail. He then told the sheriff of Schmid's confession to Bailey. Sheriff Burr recalled that "when I lightly called the lawyer on the contradiction [of who suggested the plea], Tinney just gave a grin and I dropped the subject."

Schmid sent handwritten letters to both Bailey and Tinney, dismissing them as his attorneys, then sent a thirty-eight page writ to Judge Roylston, asking for a new trial. Schmid cited, "The use of extreme mental coercing instigated by Mr. Bailey and followed through by co-counsel Mr. Tinney, in highly persuasive and misleading tactics utilized to direct a plea of guilty on the defendant." He stated that on various occasions both attorneys had said to him 'We'll do just enough to protect the record for an appeal and nothing else. . . . You haven't a chance, Smitty, give it up. . . . You know you're guilty, you can't hold on much longer, you're a sick man. . . . Do you want to kill your mother?' "

Pleading guilty to second degree was not done by free choice, Schmid said, and Bailey had expressed a desire to "get the damned thing over with." Schmid noted the denial for change of venue and that after denying him reassurance of an effective, adequate defense, his attorneys "set about to demolish his resistance to the guilty plea," and that he agreed with them finally "out of fear, fear of an attorney possessing godlike powers of destruction," and fears of "mentally murdering my beloved parents by the ensuing litigation." Schmid said he now fully expected both Bailey and Tinney to pull out of the appeal on the Fritz case.

Then, in outlining a plan for a final move to prove his innocence, Schmid said: "By the recovery of said corpse, evidence will become apparent that death did not occur by cranium mutilation, bashing, stoning or any other direct process in which a heavy blunt object was utilized to crush the skull, but in fact occurred when Mr. Schmid heard Miss Rowe scream and returned to find her lying prone on the ground, partially stripped of clothing, and dead from the strangling effects of Mr. Saunders' hands."

Schmid said that he was aware that "Mr. Saunders suffered a severe sexual repression that resulted in his actions," but for which Schmid felt that "Saunders does not deserve to die."

Further, "The defendant gladly risks his life for an attempt to remove the fog enveloping and distorting the truth," he said. "The defendant does not ask for reappointment of counsel and will gladly accept the responsibility of defense in solitude, if necessary, thus saving the taxpayers added burden. But in the interest of truth, intrinsic to justice, grant him this opportunity to fight."

Charging that Bailey told him his case was "hopeless under sagebrush justice," Schmid accused him of a "breach of confidentiality, an irresponsible attitude and general disinterest, deceivement, and the deliberate coercing of the defendant for purposes valuable to Mr. Bailey, and detrimental to the defendant during a time in which the defendant was unable to resist."

Schmid sent a copy of the writ to the *Citizen*, waiving publication rights. "Publicity," said a reporter, "is a two-edged sword."

Tinney declined to comment on Schmid's allegations, and Bailey could not be reached.

Upon receipt of the document, Roylston said he would treat Schmid's "accusations that he was coerced into pleading guilty as a motion to withdraw his plea." He said he would hear Schmid's request for a new trial and "all other pending matters" at nine o'clock Monday morning, June 12, the time for sentencing.

Schmid contacted former Deputy County Attorney William Healy and asked him to take over his defense. Healy refused saying it would constitute a conflict of interest since he represented the county at the time the Fritz case began. Another attorney also refused the case.

Saunders' new lawyer had requested that his hearing transcript against Schmid be kept secret. Appearing before Judge Roylston, Schafer opposed this motion and also asked that Schmid's request to withdraw his guilty plea be denied, citing in his memorandum that: "Apparently the sole basis for the defendant's request . . . is the allegation that his lawyers coerced him into such a plea. Aside from a personal denouncement of Mr. Bailey, the defendant in no way shows that anyone forced him to plead guilty. Schmid not only told the court that he had not been coerced or promised anything, but that he had killed Alleen Rowe and that he pleaded [sic] 'because I'm guilty.'" Schafer felt that Schmid's motion to withdraw his plea "seems more an outgrowth of the realization that now he will have to pay for his own confessed acts."

In private, Schafer was still uncertain as to what had happened. He believed that Schmid would not have received the death sentence, and said, "I really can't figure out why Charlie entered that plea. Without the body, I wouldn't have done it if I was in his place."

A man who "grew airsick at the thought of flight," Schafer kept thinking of one witness in Kansas City he had flown twice to interview during his preparation for the Rowe trial. With an astonished look, Schafer said, "Neither Bailey nor Tinney seemed interested in what my witnesses were going to say. They didn't even question them. Bailey asked me to write up what my witnesses were going to say and he'd stipulate to all of it. 'All of it?' I asked him. He said, 'Sure, just write it up.' It took me about three hours to type it up and he stipulated to it."

Sometime before the trial began, Schafer had telephoned county attorneys in other states to consult with them concerning the Boston attorney. "Now," Schafer said, "he seemed to have other things on his mind. He was tricky but it was all surface." According to Schafer, he felt that if he had put up a fight, he would only have camouflaged Bailey's inadequacy. "Here I was planning for a war, and I didn't even get an argument," Schafer said. "So I let him play it out on his own." But the prosecutor had not counted on such an abrupt halt to the activity. "When they asked me if I'd take second degree, I thought 'Holy cow, do they realize what they're doing?' I didn't believe them, and I didn't let on that I was shocked. So I sort of sat back and waited for whatever was going to happen."

Since the trial, Tinney had publicly praised Schafer's handling of the case, saying that each time a defense motion was made Schafer had one or more legal citations to support the state's position.

The court finally appointed attorney William Scanland to represent Schmid's interests, and he appeared with Schmid on June 19, for sentencing.

Judge Roylston first questioned two psychiatrists, Dr. Cutts and Dr. Abbuhl. Both testified that in their opinion the defendant knew "right from wrong," knew the nature and quality of his acts, and was mentally able to assist counsel in his own behalf.

When asked whether Schmid knew the nature of the proceedings against him when he made his plea, Dr. Cutts replied that he had no definite opinion and "could only make an educated guess."

Replying to the same question, Dr. Abbuhl said that Schmid "probably did understand the nature of the proceedings against him on May 20. . . ." He said that he had talked to Schmid twice, "for about forty-five minutes the first time on May 29, and for about an hour the second time on June 5." Answering a question from Scanland, Dr. Abbuhl said that Schmid had refused to submit to psychological tests. Judge Roylston interjected that Schmid had also refused to submit to tests from court-appointed psychologists on two occasions.

After the two psychiatrists had finished testifying, Judge Roylston said that he was prepared to hear Schmid's motion to withdraw his guilty plea. Scanland promptly announced that the defendant "asks that his motion be abandoned and withdrawn."

Roylston asked Schmid if there had been any promises or threats made in connection with his decision to withdraw his motion. Schmid paused for a few seconds, shook his head and murmured "No." Asked if his decision was voluntary, he wiped his nose with the back of his sleeve and said, "Yes. . . ."

Then Scanland asked that Schmid's "writ to withdraw his plea be stricken from the record and destroyed."

The judge denied the request to destroy the document and ordered it sealed, "not to be opened except by order of the court."

Referring to the psychiatric hearing, that Schmid was legally sane, the judge ruled that the defendant was eligible for sentence. "Is there anything you wish to advise the court of before sentencing, Mr. Scanland?"

The attorney asked for court appointment of other psychiatrists for further examinations, but the request was denied. Judge Roylston then asked if there was any legal reason why Schmid should not be sentenced. Scanland said the only other reason would be "for a presentence hearing for mitigation."

"I will consider any matters for mitigation at this time," the judge said, but Scanland replied that he had "nothing at this time." Judge Roylston then asked Schmid if he had anything to say before sentence was passed upon him.

Schmid stood up so abruptly it started Scanland. His face twitching slightly, he said, "No."

Roylston then pronounced the sentence. Fifty years to life imprisonment at the Arizona State Penitentiary.

Tears in his eyes, in a barely audible voice, Schmid asked the judge if he could reject the sentence.

"I would prefer death."

There was no statutory provision for rejecting the sentence. Schmid was handcuffed and led from the courtroom.

Under this sentence, Schafer said, Schmid would be

eligible for parole in about thirty years, and with the Rowe case concluded (minus the body), the prosecution moved ahead to oppose anticipated litigation in the appeal of Schmid's death sentences in the Fritz case. Schafer asserted that Schmid's withdrawal of the coercion claim might hurt his appeal in the Fritz case. "The next step for us," Schafer said, "is the Fritz appeal. We will now await the filing of the defense's initial brief. We don't know exactly what we will have to respond to until we see their brief. But we do know from the first trial that one of the main contentions was the connection between the Fritz and Rowe cases. . . . The defendant claimed at that time [during the Fritz trial], that he had not killed the Rowe girl, thus making no reason for killing Gretchen." The county attorney then emphasized: "He has not only pleaded guilty and been sentenced for killing Miss Rowe, but there is no doubt whatsoever that he did kill the Rowe girl. The withdrawal of the motion that he was coerced into pleading guilty removed all doubt from the matter."

But Schafer still wondered about the development of Schmid's guilty plea. He asked a confidant of Schmid's, and was told: "It wasn't difficult. Schmid was convinced that *you* had offered the deal in hopes of ending a costly trial, that you were being fair as it would be his only way to escape the gas. If he didn't accept your deal, he'd be dead in ninety days."

"How would he be dead?" Schafer asked.

"Because of the introduction of the Fritz case into the

Rowe trial. He was led to understand that such evidence would automatically kill his appeal in the Fritz case, and as a result he'd be dead in ninety days—the death sentence carried out."

Schafer looked bewildered. "I've never heard of such a thing. My god! I don't even know how something like that could *work* legally!"

Attorney Scanland, after filing notice of appeal as his last official act for Schmid, requested that he be allowed to withdraw from the case.

At the County Jail, Schmid now refused to see any visitors except Sheriff Burr and Dan Sakall. On Friday morning, June 23, 1967, Schmid told Sakall, "I want to lead the authorities to the grave of Alleen Rowe."

Sheriff Burr got in touch with Judge Roylston and received court approval to have Schmid search for the body. Two lawyers present at the jail were asked to accompany the search party as impartial witnesses. Both consented.

Wearing a white shirt, dark trousers, hands manacled in front, Schmid climbed into the back seat of a deputy's car and smoked casually as they drove to the desert area off Harrison Road.

In the blinding sunlight, Schmid walked out into the desert to an arroyo about 300 yards south of Golf Links Road and a quarter of a mile east of Harrison, accompained by Dan Sakall and the sheriff.

Schmid indicated two sites as the possible grave but subsequent digging by Schmid and a deputy uncovered nothing in those spots. Then Schmid scrambled up the slope of the wash, glanced around and pointed to a gnarled Palo Verde tree.

"That's the spot," he said. "I'm sure now."

The spot he pointed to was only 50 yards from the area John Saunders and Mary French had led police to twenty months before.

Schmid hurried across the rocky wash, carrying the shovel, and dug as well as he could with his wrists handcuffed, moving away a layer of sandy earth, then a few more shovelfulls and suddenly one knee joint was uncovered, then the pelvis of the skeleton, approximately six inches below the surface of a shallow grave.

Pathologist Edward Brucker arrived and he, Schmid, and Sakall probed the area until they uncovered the skull, the jaws parted wide and the cavity packed with sand. Three years and twenty-three days since the night of her disappearance, Alleen Rowe was finally found.

Sheriff Burr brushed the bones with a whiskbroom. Spectators were gathering. "We came as fast as we could," a woman said, "as soon as we heard there was a skeleton."

"Daddy, there's the head," a small boy said. "Where's the rest of it?"

"Don't worry," his father replied. "They'll dig it up, you'll see it," and hoisted the boy onto his shoulders so he could see the grave.

On his knees, Schmid cradled the skull in his hands and said excitedly to Brucker, "You see? There's no cranium damage, no contusions to the skull. . . ."

The rubber soles of the tennis shoes on the feet of the skeleton had rotted, but her black bathing suit was well preserved. Reporters and newsmen started to arrive and television cameramen shot closeups of the skull. Burr held the skull in his hand for the cameras, then passed it to Walter Birkby, an anthropologist from the university, who said he couldn't tell immediately if the skull had been fractured.

"There's no fractures," Schmid insisted, squatting alongside Burr and the pathologist. Schmid stood up and stared at a man holding a child and said pointedly, "I think it's shameful that people bring kids to see a thing like this."

Brucker disjoined the lower jaw from the skull, then placed all the bones into three cardboard boxes.

By Saturday morning, an autopsy and detailed X-rays revealed fractures at the base of the skull. There was no evidence of damage to the cervical vertebrae. The area around the fractures was coated with dried blood, indicating that the fractures were induced while Alleen Rowe was still alive. A rock found near the skull was also examined and blood specks were found on its sharp end. The rock was included in the closetful of papers and accumulated objects that made up the closed Rowe file.

Quietly, Sheriff Burr said, "Charlie doesn't have any

regrets about anything he's done, he doesn't feel sorrow, not even remorse. I don't even think he feels pain. He doesn't like anybody, and says that he has no close ties with anybody. He says he never, never has been close to anyone."

Epilogue

THE DAY SCHMID uncovered the body, I received a phone call late at night from a television newsman I knew. The films of Schmid showing the grave and Burr holding up the skull had appeared on the evening news. "So Burr and Sakall wooed old Charlie," the newsman said. "I figured they'd convince him that only *he* could set the record straight. They must have worked pretty skillfully on him . . ."

It had come to an end, all but the appeals and the waiting, perhaps the years of reviewing the volumes of transcripts that included some twenty-odd books of pretrial publicity. But it was over.

A few days later I saw Schmid at the penitentiary. He was playing badminton with three other Death

Row inmates. I spoke to him through the high fence. He looked different. Smaller, older perhaps.

"I'm not stupid," he said. "If I had known her head was broken like that I would never have taken them out there." The difference I'd noticed was especially true of his eyes. They were clearer, but they still betrayed nothing of whatever he felt. As he absently thrust the handle of his racket through the mesh of the fence, he smiled slightly and said, "If I did it, I'd like to find out why—the answer might help somebody else."